"BACK OF THE NAPKIN"

Buying, Selling and Leasing

Commercial Real Estate Simplified

With Bonus Sales Technique Material

Philip A. Okun

Back Of the Napkin

ISBN: 978-1-917306-63-8

In Memory

Steve Harney

1955-2024

A great partner, friend, and person.

You are missed!

Dedication

As of the writing of this book, the coronavirus has turned the world upside down. This is an unprecedented time that we hope will never repeat itself. This book is dedicated to the true heroes of this crisis. Namely, all the front-line medical workers, EMTs, firefighters, police, grocery store employees and all those tireless individuals trying to keep the supply chain working and all of us well and safe.

Again, thank you all!

Acknowledgments

In all our lives, certain individuals have had the most influence on us. There have been several positive influencers for me, but the most important is my wife, Linda. She has had an enormous impact on me with unconditional love, support, encouragement, and a constant belief that "you can do this!" Many times, she convinced me to "go further" and "do more". She was right! Every time I listened; I was rewarded! I am especially rewarded because she is my best friend and soul mate. Thank you for that and so many other things!

I am also blessed to have a great family. My parents, Harold and Theda, were two very special people; they loved me and my brother Alan unconditionally and gave us tremendous support in our endeavors. My brother Alan is a great brother and he and his fabulous wife Susan are always there for us.

Adam and Jaime, Linda's two incredible sons, have also been a source of love and encouragement virtually since I met them in 1990. Sadly, Jaime has left us way too soon. I feel his spirit all the time and hear the typical things he used to say to me often. I admired his ability and desire to constantly give of himself to others. Jaime used to say, "The greatest gift you can give to others is time." This he did, working with foster kids, after-school programs and doing volunteer work with animals. Adam is a powerhouse of energy and commitment. His work ethic is an inspiration to me. I thoroughly enjoy our talks and getting insight into how he sees the world. His entrepreneurial spirit and drive will take him anywhere he wants to go.

Throughout my career, I have had my "village of influencers" that helped shape my thinking and forced me to constantly raise my game. Kevin McClarnon, Steve Harney, who are the best partners one can have, and my original mentor, Bill Bendernagel, who started me down this path. Michael Puorro, CEO of Hanover Bank and John Fitzgerald, President of Realty Connect USA Long Island are also part of that village. Mike's leadership skills are awe inspiring, and he has helped me grow as a bank director, which is a role I truly enjoy. John's dedication to every sales agent in the company is, in my view, unique to the industry.

I also need to acknowledge my Back of The Napkin colleague and dear friend, Ron Epstein. We spend hours analyzing and reanalyzing deal after deal. His talent for analytics and his knowledge of this business is astounding. We approach things differently, but somehow, we always get to where we need to be. He is one of the smartest people I know and a truly valued friend and sounding board.

Last, but not least a special thanks to our dear friends, Bob and Cheryl Burghardt, who have been with us through thick and thin. We love you both!

Author's Note

As you know from reading my dedication, when I began writing this book, we were in the middle of the worst pandemic in 100 years. As we are preparing to go to publication, we are experiencing a crisis in commercial real estate, especially with urban office properties. Work from home, which was necessitated by the covid-19 pandemic has had a lasting impact as people are still reluctant to go back to the office. Downtown office properties are experiencing very high vacancy rates causing loss of cash flow and diminution of values, in many cases to the point where these properties are worth less than the debt.

I am dating myself here, but I have been through numerous banking and real estate crises, starting with the Tax Reform Act of 1986, (TRA86) which changed the rules of the game regarding, among other things, limited partnerships, and passive income, in the middle of the game. TRA86 helped precipitate the savings and loan crisis and a recession in the early 1990's. I experienced interest rates as high as 16%, a period of no money available to borrow at any rate, the great recession of 2008 and most recently a string of bank failures, such as Signature Bank, and Silicon Valley Bank.

What I can tell you is that each time there was a crisis we ended up getting through it and commercial real estate was all the stronger. One thing I can tell you about the larger commercial real estate owners is that they are incredibly resilient. In my view you'll see repurposing of distressed properties and a genesis that will take commercial real estate to the next level. With the advent of ecommerce, the pundits were sounding the death knell of brick-and-mortar retail. Never happened. Another trait of major top developers and owners is their creativity. I have seen this repeatedly in my own experiences and my observations of other owners/developers. Of course, there will always be some casualties as the weaker owners may not have the staying power to get to the other side. Those properties will ultimately get absorbed as well.

If we learn from failures it leads to greater success. I have an expression: Attitude is Altitude. It works both ways. Low attitude, low altitude. Keep your attitude high as much of the time that you can, and I promise you high altitude!

Table of Contents

Foreword

There is an expression many of you may know: "Back of The Napkin". This refers to a causal analysis of basically anything. Story has it that "The Laffer Curve", which claims to show the relationship between tax cuts and government income, was drawn by Arthur Laffer in 1974 on a bar napkin to show an aide to President Gerald R. Ford why the federal government should cut taxes.

In this book, "Back of The Napkin" refers to commercial real estate. Let us say you are discussing with a business associate the value of a shopping center at the hotel bar. You pull out your pen, and your cell phone (who uses a calculator anymore?), and nearby there is certainly an abundance of----you got it----bar napkins! Now, I am not too sure why we can't use the front of the napkin because it, too, is usually blank unless it has an ad of some sort, which is kind of tacky, but nonetheless, we turn it over to the back just to stay true to the name. (I guess that implies the analysis is even more casual than using the front of the napkin, but I digress.) You then proceed to write down some basic information, *forget the pencil,* as you can't erase it on a napkin, as it will shred, and you proceed to do a simple analysis, which I will teach you, in order to arrive at a value. No question you can find as many sophisticated and complicated analyses' as there are days in a year. I choose to look at things more simply. Many people feel the same way. We don't want our brains to be in pain, just trying to figure out what a property is worth. We just want to "get it" and get it quickly. There is no argument that a more scientific and sophisticated analysis will create a more exacting result. The simple reality is that at the end of the day, the marketplace will determine the value of any property regardless of the 140-page spreadsheet that analyzes future value, discounted cash flow, present value, discounted present value, internal rate of return and a host of other "commercial babble" jargon that in my view, will get you nowhere. I am not trying to denigrate all the educational institutions that teach this stuff (well, maybe I am), but the simple reality is that after 40-plus years of going to this rodeo, I can get you there much quicker and easier. At this stage of my life, I get pure joy and satisfaction by sharing with others. I have been blessed with a more than reasonable level of success and continue to do so with my work as a partner at Realty Connect USA on Long Island, where I assist agents who want to learn and succeed in commercial real estate. Whether it's office, industrial, retail, land, investments, Main Street or High Street, been there, done that, I will share all of this with you. I have had my share of wins and losses, but either way, you learn for the next time.

Additionally, I serve as a founding director and chairman of the credit committee for Hanover Bank, also on Long Island. In that capacity, I have been involved in the approval of hundreds of millions of dollars in commercial real estate loans. I will share these experiences to help you get your loans closed effectively and as quickly as possible. The goal of this book, and you will hear a lot about GOALS in a bit, is to help you understand any aspect of commercial real estate quickly and clearly by using 'The Back of The Napkin'. We will cover office and industrial, leasing and sales, land analysis, retail leasing and sales, investment property analysis and Main Street property leasing and sales. We won't leave anything out. Everything you need, including all forms discussed in this book, are available for free at www.backofthenapkin.biz. Also, feel free to contact me anytime at philip@philipokun.com with any questions at all.

It's All In the Setup

Back of the Napkin is very simple if you are prepared. What that means is that before you turn that napkin over and start to analyze, you want to have all the pieces of the puzzle necessary. Many years ago, I took a course preparing to take my Coast Guard Captains license exam. The teacher, who was a true old salt and just as crusty, taught me one of the most valuable lessons of my life. I have applied this to almost everything I do and think of him every time I use it. He said, at least 10 times in each class, *"It's all in the setup. You can successfully complete every task if you start with the proper items."* We were learning to plot a course from point A to point B using the then necessary paper charts. In order to plot a course, one needed certain formulas, nautical charts, a parallel ruler, dividers and a pencil. The details of these items are not important. What is important is that you do not sit down to tackle the problem unless you have everything prepared. Further, he said, "The FIRST thing you do is write down the formulas you will need to use. Do not rely on your memory because that is when mistakes happen. Simply write them down so you can refer to them as you go through the plotting question. He could not have been more correct. Once well setup, the execution is merely following "The bouncing ball". The plotting questions on the Coast Guard exam are anything but simple. Following his advice, I got 10 out of 10 correct. It truly was all in the setup.

The same applies to commercial real estate, or anything else for that matter. For every type of property, there are specific items that you will need BEFORE you try to assess and value a property. I will provide specific checklists for every type of commercial property so you can accurately do the analysis. As in chart plotting, there are specific formulas you will need to learn. Each property type has what I call a "Holy Grail." This is the one thing that you just cannot do without. By the time you finish this book, you will understand all of them and have the ability to do The Back of The Napkin with confidence.

Goals

In the introduction, I mentioned goals, which you would hear a lot about. This is the time to address them, as goals are part of the Setup. (Remember, it's all in the setup.) Yogi Berra was (possibly incorrectly) quoted as saying, "If you don't know where you are going, you won't know when you get there." How true those words are.

Before I start any meeting, teach any class, or make any phone call (business or personal), I mentally establish the goal. It makes no sense to start any interaction without knowing what you hope to accomplish. Other than a casual chit-chat conversation, it is important to establish the goal ahead of time. Doing so creates a clearer road map so that you can gauge whether you were successful or not. Determining your goal before any phone call or meeting initially requires intentional effort to do so. Over time, it becomes automatic. Back in the day, before I made a phone call, I would put my hand on this thing called a receiver, which in those days was the part of the telephone you spoke into. Before I would dial a number, yes, dial, I would ask myself, "What do you want to accomplish on this call?" Once I was satisfied with my answer, I would proceed to make the call. That was many years ago, and over time, my "mini-goal setting" as I call it, became automatic. I have literally trained somewhere north of 1,000 commercial real estate agents in my 40+ years. One of the first things I do is hold a class on goal setting and then individual meetings to discuss personalized goals.

A good "road map" is essential, and you start the creation process by defining your 'Why'. We all have a 'why': "Because I need to provide for my family", "because I want the freedom to manage my life my way", "because I want to travel more", "because I want to retire at 50."

No matter your 'Why', you need to identify it and be true to yourself. You must then set your goals: "I want to own 3 commercial properties within 24 months." "I want to broker 10 office leases in the next 12 months." Your goals will vary depending on whether you are a broker, investor, or tenant. Either way, you need goals. For a goal to be valid, it needs to pass 3 tests: A goal must be measurable, realistic, and challenging. 2 out of 3 does not cut it. 3 for 3 is the passing grade. Let us look at these closely. "I want to make 1 million dollars buying and selling commercial property in the next 12 months." Is it measurable? Yes. Is it challenging? Maybe. Is it realistic? Maybe. You need to look at your own history to determine that. If you are just starting out, then there is no question it's measurable and challenging but most likely not realistic. Using your own track record, you can determine whether any goal meets all 3 tests. Measurable, realistic, and challenging. ALL 3. Measurable is the simple part, as you can quantify any goal with numbers or some other barometer of success. The tricky part is finding the balance between challenging and realistic. If the goal is too easy, you will not grow. If it is too ambitious, you will not reach the goal, thereby setting yourself up for disappointment. You need a plan once you establish your why and set some goals. Goals without a plan are just wishes. Your plan needs to be written. Once it is written, you have a base to work from. The next thing you need to do is share the plan. It could be your spouse or significant other, a friend, a business partner, or anyone that you trust and have respect for their input and opinions. This creates accountability. Sometimes, that will put you in an uncomfortable place, especially when the plan is not working. Nonetheless, you must face the music, especially to yourself. The plan is certainly subject to modification as all plans are imperfect. As you progress, you will need to review the plan, change things that are not working, and add or remove certain tasks. You need to be flexible and honest in assessing the success or failure of a plan. The assessment process needs to be ongoing, as you can't wait a year to realize that your plan is not working. Consider monthly reviews in the beginning, as you may need to make adjustments so you don't get too far off course. Eventually, you can visit the plan quarterly once you are comfortable with the progress.

The plan needs to contain a series of tasks that will enable you to reach your goals. If one of your goals is to acquire 3 investment properties in the next 12 months, you need to establish what it will take to find, analyze, and acquire those properties. There are tasks like internet research, maybe driving a market to look for the type of property you want to acquire, and meeting with brokers who specialize in your desired area. A plan would include fixed periods that you dedicate to those tasks. Those tasks are like mini-goals you need to accomplish to realize the big goals you seek. "I will speak to a minimum of 5 property owners each week in order to find at least one potential prospect." That in and of itself is a goal. Test it to see. Is it measurable? Yes. A minimum of 5. Is it realistic? I would say so. Is it challenging? Again, I would say it probably is. If it turns out it was too easy, then you can modify it upward. This is where the assessment and flexibility come into play. Constantly tweaking tasks to increase the ones that work and decreasing or even eliminating things that don't.

Back of The Napkin-

Investment Properties

An investment property is any property that creates an income stream or has the potential to do so. The basics are the same whether it is a 2-store strip center or a 1 million square foot mall. Back of the Napkin probably works best for investment properties because of the consistency of the analysis. This would include shopping centers, office buildings, industrial buildings, multi-family properties, and mixed-use properties that are being purchased as an investment, not by an owner/user. The owner/user is a completely different analysis and will be covered separately. That said, investment properties can be the most complex to analyze if you choose to go that route, other than maybe land, which also has many moving parts. As I said in the introduction, many different matrixes are commonly used to analyze investment properties.

Referring to *"It's All in the Setup"* let's establish what we need <u>before</u> we attempt to use Back of the Napkin. Again, this list is the same for any investment property. The only variation is if we are analyzing an empty building to be potentially used as an investment property, as you will see.

OK, here is what we need for the setup:

1. An accurate rent roll. (form available on www.backofthenapkin.biz) This would include the size of each unit, the tenant name, and use, the start date, the expiration date, annual increases in rent, a breakdown of any options to renew the lease, any additional expenses that the tenant is responsible for, the rent per square foot (except for apartments), the annual gross rent being paid and, optionally, the monthly rent being paid by each tenant. If the building is vacant or partially vacant, then you would need to make rental assumptions based on the market you are in. Research can be done to determine the current rent per square foot for that particular property type.

2. An accurate income and expense statement. (form available on www.backofthenapkin.biz) We need a complete breakdown of ALL property operating expenses, including but not limited to: real estate taxes, property insurance, snow removal, landscaping, utilities that the landlord is responsible for, repairs and maintenance, and management fees, to name a few. Completeness of

expenses is paramount. Debt service payments are not considered an operating expense. If you are looking to purchase a property or list one if you are a broker, the last thing you want is any surprises down the road. Again, assumptions will need to be made if the property is vacant or partially vacant.

A copy of the survey, if available. If not, then the size of the land area in total and the number of linear feet frontage on the main road the property fronts on.

Once we have all of this, we can begin our analysis. In its most basic form back of the napkin takes the gross income minus expenses which leaves us with what is called net operating income, or NOI. The NOI is simply the net income, or the potential net income, that is, or can be, derived from the property. Debt service from a mortgage is not subtracted as an operating expense. The NOI is the *Holy Grail* for investment properties, as it is the single most important number for the analysis. If the NOI is wrong the value will be wrong. Not just a "little" wrong, but BIG wrong. You will see why in a minute. Let us take a step back and illustrate what we have so far.

First we look at the rent roll:

Rent Roll

Property Address:

123 Main Street, Anytown

Tenant	Size (sq. ft.)	Lease Start	Lease End	Base Rent (annual)	Base Rent (per. Sq. foot.)	Increases	Option(s)?	Utilities
Dr. Davis, DDS	2,200	1/1/2010	12/31/2030	$65,040	$29.56	3%	no	sep meter
Orbit Architects	408	3/31/2015	2/28/2025	$12,768	$31.29	3%	no	sep meter
Dave Wilson, CPA	900	2/1/2020	1/30/2025	$21,300	$23.88	3%	no	sep meter
Dance Wonder	3,000	1/1/1990	2/28/2029	$58,296	19.43	3%	no	sep meter
Apartment 1	1,000	4/1/2023	3/30/2024	$22,200	22.2	0	no	sep meter
Apartment 2	992	6/1/2022	5/30/2029	$23,396	23.58	3%	no	sep meter
Totals	8,500			$203,000				

From the rent roll, we know the following necessary facts for the analysis:

The gross rental income is: $203,000.

The gross leasable area of the property is: 8,500 square feet.

Examining the rent roll also tells us many other things. You can detect the fact that there is upside potential in this property by looking at the rent per sq. foot column. The dance studio is clearly below the other tenants rent per foot, which likely indicates he is below market. We also see the CPA expires in 2025 and his rent is also below 2 of the tenants.

We now proceed to look at the income/expense statement:

Income & Expense Statement

Subject Property:
123 Main Street, Anytow   8,500 sf

Income		
Base Rent	$	203,000
Tax Reimbursements	$	5,000
Total income	**$**	**208,000**

Expenses		
Taxes	$	31,050
Insurance	$	15,037
Utilities	$	7,800
Landscaping/Snow Removal	$	1,500
Rubbish Removal	$	1,800
Repairs/Maintenance	$	5,000
Managememnt Fees	$	10,400
Professional Fees	$	2,000
Vacancy		
Total Expenses	**$**	**74,587**

Net Operating Income	$	133,413

From the income/expense statement, we know the following necessary facts for the analysis:

The gross rental income (transferred from the rent roll) is: $203,000. There are tax reimbursements of $5,000, which results in gross income of $208,000.

The total operating expenses are: $74,587.

When you subtract the total operating expenses from the gross income you are left with net operating income, or NOI. This is the "Holy Grail" of investment properties. (Have I made that point?) It ALL begins and ends with the NOI.

Going back to the $5,000 in tax reimbursements, 2 of the leases provide for real estate tax reimbursements. In this case, they each pay their pro-rata share of the real estate tax increases over the base year in their leases. For example, if a tenant occupies 20% of the total space of the building, the tenant would be responsible for 20% of the tax increase. If the base year taxes in the tenant's lease are $10,000 and the new taxes are $13,000, the tenant would be responsible for 20% of $3,000, which would be $600.

There are 2 categories of expenses you need to be aware of. The first is management fees, which are not shown on many income/expense statements as owners can, and often do, self-manage the property and, therefore, not pay a third-party management fee. The second is known as the vacancy factor, which is rarely seen on an income/expense statement. This is a deduction of a percentage of the income, usually around 7-10% of the gross income. Even if the property is fully leased, this becomes a consideration if financing is being used to purchase the property. Banks will underwrite the loan, deducting a management fee and vacancy factor, as they are looking to protect their downside. Banks do not generally manage properties, so they would need to hire a third-party management company if they took the property through foreclosure. Keep in mind that debt service is not considered an operating expense. Debt is deducted after determining the net operating income (NOI).

Having an accurate NOI is paramount. Have I made that point as well? Once we have the NOI, we need to apply a capitalization rate (CAP rate) to the NOI to establish the property value. Simply put, the CAP rate is a rate of return that an investor is willing to accept. If an investor is willing to accept a 7% return, for argument's sake, then the investor would be willing to pay a price that would then yield a 7% return after subtracting operating expenses. There is a simple formula that you would use to establish that value: NOI/CAP rate=Value. The CAP rate used is a function of a particular market and property type;

we will get into more detail on that. Using 123 Main Street as our example:

Net Operating Income = $133,413

CAP Rate=7%

$133,413/.07= $1,905,900 value. This means that having paid $1,905,900 will yield an investor a 7% return before debt.

Here is what the back of the napkin would look like at its simplest level.

Gross income	$208,000
Expenses	$74,587
NOI	$133,413
	/
	.07
Value	$1,905,900

That is it! Oversimplified? To some degree, yes, but a great starting point. We need to talk about factors that will affect this valuation, negatively or positively, but at the end of the day, you at least have a firm starting point without all the brain damage. You can run 5 or 10-year projections, calculate the internal rate of return, and myriad other calculations until you are blue in the face, but I can tell you from 40+ years of experience this has worked for me. I have purchased numerous investment properties over the years, and I was a partner in a company that purchased hundreds of millions of dollars of investment real estate, and this was always my starting point.

Let us talk about the CAP rate at this point. Unlike NOI, which needs to be accurate and can be by its nature, the CAP rate is going to vary depending on a number of factors like property type, location, mortgage interest rates, market and political influences, and comparison to other investment returns, like bonds, for example.

Broad stroke, we can take a look at CAP rates as they stand, say in the northeast, as of the writing of this book in 2022. You will need to research CAP rates depending on when and where you read this book. A good commercial appraiser is the best source of CAP rates. Whether you are an investor or a broker, you need a good relationship with some local commercial real estate appraisers. A good banking relationship is also a good source of CAP rates. When determining the potential value of a property using a CAP rate, it is important to keep in mind that there is a certain subjective nature to CAP rates. 2 appraisers appraising the same property can and sometimes do apply a different CAP rate. One appraiser might use a 5.5% CAP rate, while another appraiser may use 6%. Neither one is necessarily right or wrong, as this number is not absolute. I always suggest using a range of values when analyzing a property. Using a 1% CAP rate spread is a safe way to analyze. If we take our example of $133,413 NOI from the previous example, then the indicated range based on a 6-7% CAP rate spread would be a value range of $2,223,500 at the 6% CAP and $1,905,900 at the 7% CAP rate. As you can see, 1% can make quite a difference in value. Depending on whether you are buying or selling a property, you will choose to see this most advantageously based on your goals.

Now, I will get you a little confused, but I promise to make you comfortable by the end of this dialogue. As I said earlier CAP rate is a rate of return that an investor is willing to accept. The lower the CAP rate (rate of return investors will accept), the higher the price. Ok, don't shoot! If an investor is willing to accept a 4% return on investment, that investor will pay more than an investor willing to accept, say a 7% return. Let us use $120,000 as our NOI. If investor 1 is willing to accept a 6% return, the price that the investor would be willing to pay will be as follows, assuming a property with a NOI of $120,000:

$120,000/.06= $2,000,000

If investor 2 insists on a 7% return, then the price will be as follows:

$120,000/.07= $1,714,285.

BIG difference based on the return that an investor is willing to accept. The same NOI creates a difference of nearly $300,000 based on the return that an investor will live with. Less return=higher price.

CAP rates, in general, are lower when analyzing multi-family investments. The definition of multi-family is greater than 4 residential units. 1-4 family units is considered residential real estate. Anything over 4 units is considered commercial real estate when dealing with financing. We will cover financing in depth later. The reason CAP rates are lower on multi-family is because that type of property is more desirable because there is less risk. Historically, multi-family is one of the safest investments, hence the willingness of investors to live with a lower return. I remind you of the old adage, low risk-low return, high risk-high return.

For example, currently (in 2022), multi-family investments in this region are between 4-5.5% CAP rate depending on property size (the more units, the better), location, and property condition. The more deferred maintenance needed the lower the value.

Office buildings, shopping centers, and tenanted industrial buildings sell between 6-7.5% CAP rate. Keep in mind a CAP rate is a snapshot in time and place. CAP rates will vary greatly from region to region and are also tied to the general state of the economy and interest rates. Higher rates will have a negative effect on CAP rates, as valuations will generally decrease as debt service eats up more of the cash flow of the property.

As I said earlier, an investor would look at each investment type and analyze the return they are aiming for versus the risk they are willing to take.

Back of The Napkin Snapshot

Back of the Napkin Snapshot

	Bayshore Medical	Size		7,000
	Rent Per Sq. Ft.		25 $	25.00

Income			
	Annual Base Rent	$	175,000
	Tax Reimbursements		
Total income		$	175,000

Expenses			
	Taxes	$	45,000
	Insurance	$	8,000
	Utilities	$	3,000
	Landscaping	$	2,500
	Snow Removal	$	2,000
	Repairs/Maintenance	$	4,000
	Managememnt Fees	$	8,000
	Professional Fees	$	2,000
	Vacancy	$	8,000
Total Expenses		$	82,500

Potential Value

5.5 CAP	$	1,681,818
6.5 CAP	$	1,423,077
7.0 CAP	$	1,321,429

Net Operating Income	$	92,500

The above spreadsheet was designed to create a simple snapshot of an investment property. It is basically an income/expense statement plus 3 lines for CAP rates that will automatically calculate the value range based on the

CAP rates you choose. The active spreadsheet is available at www.backofthenapkin.biz You can plug in all income and expense numbers and modify the CAP rate to any number you like, and the values will automatically recalculate.

Upside Potential

Let us spend some time on what is called upside potential. This can be important in our Back of the Napkin analysis as upside potential is the potential value that needs to be taken into account if one is going to accurately value a property. Upside potential takes many forms:

Expansion Potential: If a 5,000-square-foot building sits on 1.5 acres of land, then it is conceivable that the rentable square footage of the property can be increased. This can occur by expanding the footprint of the building or by adding additional floor(s). When we talk about land development, we will come back to this as analyzing the value of vacant land is the same analysis as analyzing expansion potential. Just keep in mind that no investor is willing to pay 100% of the upside potential value as the investor is going to be assuming the cost and risk of adding the additional potential footage.

Under Market Rent Leases: When doing any investment property analysis, it is critical to determine the approximate market rents for the type of space you are leasing in that property. If it is an office building, you need to analyze office rates for the market. If retail, then retail leases need to be researched. You will need to determine the market rent per square foot for the type of property you are potentially purchasing. Rent per foot, as we will discuss in more detail in the rental section of this book, is the holy grail of leasing. Let's say you look at a retail property that has average rental rates of $20.00 per square foot, and through your market research, you determine that the average market rents are, say, $24.00 per square foot. Let's also assume that the property has 10,000 square feet of rentable space. That would indicate that there is up to $40,000 in potential upside income. A 6% CAP rate would indicate over $650,000 in potential upside value. Granted, depending on lease lengths and tenant strength, it may take some time to get there, but still, that is the potential value that needs to be realized.

Poorly Structured Leases: Sadly, through the years, I have seen some atrocious leases supposedly drafted by competent counsel. While most lawyers are good at their craft, some simply don't understand the nuances of commercial real estate leases. One of the biggest culprits is the "Gross Lease". This is a lease where all rent and additional costs, such as taxes and maintenance fees, are included, or built into the rent. The problem is that sometimes, these leases do not provide for tenants to pay items like tax increases over a base year or increases in maintenance costs. These items add up to significant loss of potential value. In a 50,000-square-foot office building, even leaving $1.00 per foot on the table would equate to a loss of potential value of $833,000 at a 6% CAP rate ($1.00 X 50,000 square feet=$50,000/.06=$833,333). That is an enormous loss of potential value. That is just one example of the many lease flaws that could hurt value. The good news is that all leases eventually expire, which gives the new owner another bite at the apple. You MUST have a competent attorney review all leases, regardless of your experience level. There is too much at stake to be penny-wise and pound-foolish.

Main Street Properties

For any of you considering purchasing commercial real estate for the first time, I can strongly recommend cutting your teeth on Main Street properties. These are typically on a "Main Street", though not necessarily on Main Street, and will be typically between 3 and 12,000 square feet. This is approximate and will vary by market. I will use the word typically often in this section, as I need to generalize to draw a picture for you. I like this type of property and have owned a few through the years for a number of reasons. Firstly, they are usually multi-tenanted. This mitigates risk as if you lose a particular tenant, cash flow should hopefully remain positive until you replace the tenant. A particular property I own is approximately 8,500 feet. There are 4 stores/offices on the ground level and 2 apartments upstairs. Main Street apartments, in my experience, are gold. In over 20 years, I never went more than a month without replacing a tenant, and always for higher rent than the tenant that vacated was paying. In my case, another big plus is the existence of a municipal parking lot behind my property. Depending on the market you are in, a property like this will cost anywhere from $600,000 to, say, $3,000,000, depending on the size and income of the property. Smaller investment properties are few and far between. This is pretty much entry-level in the commercial real estate world. They can provide steady cash flow, with rents that typically escalate annually.

Back Of The Napkin Summary-Investment Properties

The Holy Grail for investment properties is the Net Operating Income (NOI). This is simply the gross income minus operating expenses. Debt is not considered an operating expense and, therefore, is not deducted from income to establish the NOI. You need a complete rent roll for a rented property or a projected rent roll if the property is not leased. You should research the market to establish if the rents per foot being paid by current tenants align with the market. As will be discussed, rent per square foot is the Holy Grail of leasing, so to have an accurate value, the income needs to be consistent with the market rents. You need a thorough itemized breakdown of operating expenses. The challenge here is ensuring they are complete, as sellers tend to understate expenses (and overstate income). Next you need to establish a CAP rate range for the specific type of property in a specific market it is in. For this, an appraiser or loan officer at a bank will come in very handy. The more detail you can supply regarding tenant quality, lease lengths, and any upside potential factors will be very helpful. Try to establish a 1% range of CAP rate assumption, say 6-7%, 4-5% etc. This will help create a low to high-value range. Here again is your Back of The Napkin illustration:

Gross Income-	$750,000
Operating Expenses-	$230,000
NOI	$520,000
Value Range (6 CAP)	$8,666,666
(5 CAP)	$10,400,000

Don't forget that the higher the CAP rate, the lower the value, as the value decreases if the investor demands a higher return. As can be seen, the difference in value is huge. There is a profound difference between CAP rates, even a 1% difference. If the property is more suitable for a user than for an investor, then pricing on the higher end is warranted. This may seem counterintuitive as to how does a vacant or partially vacant property warrant a higher price? This will be covered in the owner/user section.

Referring back to "Its All in the Setup" here are your setup steps.

1. WRITE down the formulas, 2 are needed: Value=Net Operating Income/CAP Rate.

    Monthly rent X 12/store size=equals rent per square foot. You may not need this formula if rent per square foot is provided, but having it at the ready is always prudent.

2. Have a completed Rent Roll.

3. Have a completed Income/Expense form.

Back Of The Napkin Checklist-Investment Properties

__Completed Rent Roll (form available at backofthenapkin.biz)

__Copy of all Leases and amendments

__Copy of Tax Bill(s)

__Survey, if available

__Detailed Income Expense Statement (form available at backofthenapkin.biz)

__Photos-Interior/exterior

__# of Parking Spaces

__# Lot size_____

(answers in the back of the book)

1. What is the "Holy Grail" for investment properties?

2. List 2 examples of upside potential.

3. Are mortgage payments considered an operating expense?

4. What is the approximate value of a property with a NOI of $312,000 with a CAP rate of 7?

5. Can a 5 family multi-family property be financed with residential financing?

6. What are the 2 most important forms needed to analyze an investment property?

7. Referring to the rent roll for 123 Main Street, which commercial tenant is paying an under-market rent?

8. Why do banks underwrite a mortgage by deducting a management fee, even if the property is self-managed?

9. Referring to the income/expense statement of 123 Main Street, how much were the tax reimbursements?

10. If the CAP rate is reduced, what is the impact on value?

Back of The Napkin- Vacant/Partially Vacant Properties

Vacant or partially vacant building sales can go one of two ways: 1. To an investor who desires to rent up the property and create an income stream, and 2. To a user who wants to use the building for some type of business use. As we will see, the value to an investor vs. a user can be, and usually is, vastly different. Investment real estate, like any other investment, is all about the rate of return and the level of risk. If one can achieve, say, a 6% return from an investment property versus, say, a 4% investment in a bond, then the investor must weigh the plusses and minuses of each investment. Though the real estate, in this example, has a higher rate of return than the bond, the bond is liquid and may be sold in an instant if needed or desired. The real estate cannot, as the sale of real estate involves a process that involves more than the push of a button, unlike the bond. There is a certain degree of risk in both, as the real estate can lose tenants and, subsequently, cash flow. With bonds, if interest rates rise, then the value of that 4% bond will fall as investors can get new bonds at a better rate. All investments will have plusses and minuses and will be driven by an investor's appetite for reward vs. risk. In order to analyze a vacant building as an investment property, we will require the same information as we covered in the section on tenanted investment properties. We will use projections and assumptions to create the value model in this situation. We would begin by building a projected income. It is not complicated to research any given geographic area to find out what the rents are in any given location. Keep in mind you are looking to determine the potential rent per square foot for the property, as this is the barometer one uses to compare rents in different properties. Rent per month will not help you as every space size will be potentially different. Knowing that the rent of a space is $3,000 per month is meaningless without knowing how many square feet the space is. It is also critical to determine what the rent includes. In some cases, it may include items like real estate taxes. In other cases, they will not be included. In order to do an apples-to-apples comparison, one must be certain that they are comparing the rents accurately. If one has access to Costar, which is an online data website, one could easily run comparables to almost any location. If not, then some market research can be done using

Loopnet.com, which is free to search on, contact an appraiser, if possible, and literally call current vacant space owners or brokers in the area. The latter will yield asking rents vs. actual closed comps, but this information is also valuable as you can apply "discounts" to the asking rents to run your projected income models. We will walk through this in this chapter. Once we build the income model, we need to project expenses. The most significant expenses are real estate taxes, insurance, utilities, landscaping and snow removal, repairs and maintenance, and management. If you are considering purchasing a vacant building for investment purposes, you should be actively looking at all available properties for sale in that market. In that way, you will be able to get some insight as to what the expenses are for similar tenanted properties. The taxes and insurance will be known quantities for the vacant property as the current owner should be paying both of those items. Assumptions can be made for most of the other expense items, keeping in mind that you would want to estimate a bit higher than lower. Using a 5,000-square-foot building, let's begin the Back of the Napkin process. Let us assume we determine that rents in the area are running between $20 and $23 dollars per square foot. We also determine that the rents are net of real estate taxes and utilities. Landlords in the area are responsible for the balance of the operating expenses.

Let's use the more conservative rent at $20 per square foot. This would create a gross income of $100,000. Based on research of other properties, you can get a feel for what the expenses "should" run. Keep in mind that you always want to analyze the expenses on a per-square-foot basis.

(Use income expense statement)

Potential Income $100,000

Projected Annual Expenses:

Taxes- $25,000 (actual from tax bill)

Insurance- $3,000 (actual from current policy)

Utilities-   Tenant paid

Maintenance- $5,000

Professional Fees- $5,000

Management- $5,000 (5% of gross income)

Landscaping- $5,000 (including snow removal)

The total expenses are projected at approximately $48,000. The gross income is projected at $100,000. This leaves a projected net operating income (NOI) of

$52,000. We would then apply a range of CAP rates to the NOI to determine a <u>potential</u> range of value. Please note the word potential as this is a major factor when determining the ultimate purchase price.

Depending on the type and quality of tenant(s) that lease the building, the CAP rate will vary, sometimes significantly. If you lease to Starbucks, for example, the CAP rate will be much lower; hence, the value will be much higher. Remember that the CAP rate is the rate of return that a purchaser is willing to accept. The lower the rate of return acceptable to the purchaser, the higher the price. With Starbucks, an investor might be willing to live with a 5% return; hence, the CAP rate would be 5%. Based on this, the value would be NOI/CAP rate or $52,000 / .05, which would indicate a potential value of $1,040,00. If the space were leased to, say, Joes Java, a local 1-store operation, the rate of return an investor would require would be much higher as the risk is higher as well. With Starbucks, you are assured that the rental stream will continue for the full duration of the lease. Hence, lower risk, lower return. Joes Java, being a higher risk, would require a higher return to the investor, say, 8%. With a CAP rate of 8, the potential value would be $52,000/.08, indicating a potential value of $650,000. BIG difference in value, to say the least. In order to determine an accurate potential value, one would start by researching the market and the local area to determine the highest and best use of the property. If the vacant property is retail, you will look to see if the property is suitable for a credit-worthy tenant, such as a national brand like Starbucks, a national drug store chain, 7-11, or a quality fast food chain, to name a few. This type of tenant will pay a competitive rent and will help create a higher value for the property once they are in and paying rent. If that is not the case and the property would only be suitable for "local" tenants, then the potential value bar needs to be set lower.

Back of The Napkin Summary-
Vacant/Partially Vacant Properties

Everything that is discussed in the Back of The Napkin Summary-Investment property also applies here. The NOI rules the day, although it is largely assumed or pro-forma as we are dealing with potential income. You will need a rent roll and income expense statement as well. Your research will include the following:

1. Research Market rents for the area and property type.

2. Plug in all known expenses, such as Taxes and insurance.

3. Make assumptions where necessary on all other expenses that are unknown.

4. Research CAP rates for the area and property type. An appraiser can be especially helpful for this.

Keep in mind that an investor buying a partially vacant or vacant property is not going to pay full potential value. They will calculate the potential value and then discount the offer to reflect that the investor needs to put in the time and money to realize the full potential value.

Back of The Napkin Checklist-Vacant/Partially Vacant Properties

__Completed Rent Roll (form available at backofthenapkin.biz)

__Copy of all Leases and amendments (if any)

__Copy of Tax Bill(s)

__Survey, if available

__Detailed Income Expense Statement (form available at backofthenapkin.biz)

__Photos-Interior/exterior

__# of Parking Spaces

__# Lot size_____

__Pro-forma demonstrating potential value.

__List of potential tenants to be approached.

Back of The Napkin-Vacant/Partially Vacant Properties-Review

(answers in the back of the book)

1. What are the 2 ways purchasers look at Vacant/Partially Vacant properties?

2. How do you analyze the potential value of a vacant/partially vacant building?

3. Typically, will an investor of a vacant/partially vacant building pay the full potential value of a property?

4. What website is useful to research asking rents in a particular market?

Back of The Napkin-

Owner/User Properties

An owner/user will look at a property differently than an investor. Let's use a restaurant owner as our example. As you will see, his Back of the Napkin will look completely different than the investor napkin. Let's assume we have a 5,000-square-foot vacant building. Let's also assume that the market rents in the area are $30.00 per square foot. This would create a cash stream of $150,000 if the property were rented to a third-party tenant. As the lease would be "triple net" the gross income would be the net operating income (NOI). All the building operating expenses are being paid by the tenant in this case. If you capitalized this income at a 7% CAP (rate the value would be approximately $2,140,000 ($150,000/.07). To create the value range I have referenced, you would also CAP this income at, say, 6% on the assumption that a quality tenant may want the space. This would indicate a value of about $2,500,000. These would be the approximate *"potential"* values to an investor. Keep in mind that a potential investor will have the exposure of renting the building, which will take some time and possible expense as there may be a commission and possibly some work on the premises for the tenant. The Back of The Napkin for an investor in this scenario would look like this,

Potential Gross Income- $150,000 ($30.00
X 5,000 square feet

Assume 4 months lease up time- $50,000
(lost income)

Commission- $40,000 (approx.)

The $90,000 expense would not be deducted from the cash flow but instead deducted from the potential value, as it will take that expense to reach the potential full value. Therefore, the Back of The Napkin value to an investor would be approximately:

$2,140,000

-$90,000

=$2,050,000

There are other potential expenses that the purchaser could incur, such as tenant improvements and other repair items. It is somewhat arbitrary and will depend on the motivation level of the seller and the buyer, but this gives quick "ballpark' values, which is true: Back of The Napkin.

Now, let's turn to the owner/user scenario. The owner/user does not completely rely on the investment analysis of the value, although it is a barometer in this case. Instead, they are looking at the property based on the potential sales volume and subsequent profits they can make in that location. Using our restaurant example, let's assume the following:

Gross Sales		$1,000,000 per annum
Cost of Goods		40%
Gross Profit		$600,000
Payroll	$200,000	
Utilities	$30,000	
Supplies	$10,000	
Professional Fees	$7,500	
Total Expenses		$247,500
Net Profit		$352,000

Comparing apples to apples, the restaurant owner will generate double the net income that an investor would. Granted, the restaurant owner needs to also account for a salary to himself for his time, but this will vary greatly depending on how hands-on the owner is. If the restaurant owner feels strongly about the volume the location could generate, he will pay far greater for the property than an investor. Hence, the CAP: rate range. If you CAP the $150,000 NOI, under the investment scenario, at, say, 6%, the value would be $2,500,000. If the restaurant owner could truly generate $350,000+ in net profit, he would likely pay the $2,500,000. In my experience, owners/users can be very aggressive if they love a location, whether it's leasing or purchasing. National tenants, such as drug chains and fast food will often reach big time for a location they feel strongly about.

Owner/Users can also qualify for SBA financing. Though more expensive than conventional financing, SBA financing generally requires a lower down payment. Additionally, SBA financing will also fund other costs, such as fixtures and equipment. The property owner must occupy at least 51% of the property to qualify. The rest of the space can be leased to other tenants, which is an additional plus as that income will offset the expenses of the property. The section on Financing will go into greater detail.

Those considering acquiring real estate for their own use need to weigh the pros and cons of leasing vs. purchasing. There are ramifications to both, and should be considered carefully before deciding. In my Back of The Napkin way I will help you with this, as this has come up many times in my career.

Leasing gives you a certain level of flexibility as you may need to expand or contract over the years. Although there are limitations based on the fact that you are committed to a lease, most landlords will be happy to lease you a larger space if it is available. This works particularly well with office or industrial space as the specific location in a particular property is less important. Retail can be a bit more challenging, as the shopping center may be full, or no desirable spaces may be available. In general, landlords are not very keen on reducing space size, but if faced with the prospect of a tenant going out of business, they may have some flexibility. Ultimately, the lease will expire giving you the flexibility to move all together or relocate within the same property. Leasing also helps preserve capital as the cost of entry is usually a security deposit of typically 2 months' rent. On the negative side, when you lease, you are at the mercy of the landlord. Eventually, all leases expire, and the tenant's fate is in the landlord's hands. You do not control your own destiny. When purchasing a property for your own use you have peace of mind that you do control your own destiny. Purchasing will require a substantial down payment. SBA financing can help reduce the cash required, and we will cover this in financing. That said, the cash requirement will be much higher on a purchase as opposed to a lease. That being the case, there is a major consideration one needs to analyze. Let's assume you have $1,000,000 in cash at your disposal. You can either use that cash as a downpayment on a building you purchase, or you could continue to lease space and invest that capital elsewhere, whether it be in your own business, an investment piece of real estate, stocks, bonds or any other investment vehicle. You need to determine where you are best suited deploying that capital. On the next page you will see a spreadsheet that does this comparison of leasing versus owning. It's a very big decision with long-term ramifications. Once you own a building, your growth is limited by the size of the building or the amount of available space if there are other tenants in the building. In my view, owning a multi-tenanted building in which you occupy part of the space is the best-case scenario. In essence, you have the other tenants paying part or possibly all of your expenses of the property. The following spreadsheet will demonstrate this.

Lease vs. Own Analysis
123 Main Street, Anywhere USA

Building Size (square ft.)	13,500	Rent per Ft. $ 21.00	4% Annual Increases
Owner-User Space	3,670		
Additional Tenant Income	196,260		

Lease

	Annual	Rent per Ft.	After Tax Deduction
Year 1	$ 77,070	21.00	14.70
Year 2	$ 80,153	21.84	15.29
Year 3	$ 83,359	22.71	15.90
Year 4	$ 86,693	23.62	16.54
Year 5	$ 90,161	24.57	17.20
Year 6	$ 93,767	25.55	17.88
Year 7	$ 97,518	26.57	18.60
Year 8	$ 101,419	27.63	19.34
Year 9	$ 105,476	28.74	20.12
Year 10	$ 109,695	29.89	20.92
Year 11	$ 114,082	31.09	21.76
Year 12	$ 118,646	32.33	22.63
Year 13	$ 123,492	33.62	23.54
Year 14	$ 128,327	34.97	24.48
Year 15	$ 133,460	36.37	25.46
Total Rent Paid	$ 1,543,218		$ 1,080,253
Average Cost per Foot after tax deduction based on 30% tax bracket:			$ 19.62
Value at end of Lease	0		
Equity after 15 years	0		

Own

Purchase Price	$	1,700,000
Down Payment	$	900,000
Mortgage	$	800,000
Annual Debt Service	$	61,853 25 year amort 6%%
Utilities	$	42,000
Taxes	$	70,923
Insurance	$	6,243
Management Fee	$	14,274
Janitorial	$	15,460
Other Expenses	$	10,000
Annual Carry Total	$	220,753
Annual Carry per ft.	$	16.35
Less Depreciation	$	34,871.79
Effective Reduction	$	24,410 based on 30% tax bracket
Savings per Foot	$	1.81 tax bracket
Net Depreciation	$	16.35
	$	1.81
Additional Tenant Inc.	$	14.53
Effective Carry per Foot	$	0.01
Sale in Yr. 15	$	7,468,511
Mortgage balance yr. 15	$	464,275
Net Equity after 15 years	$	2,004,236

Value Schedule

Based on Moodys and Real Capital Analytics. Historically
Shows 14 year average increase in value of 5.4%
This model assumes half of the actual historical increase- 2.7%

Year 1	$	1,700,000
Year 2	$	1,745,900
Year 3	$	1,793,039
Year 4	$	1,841,451
Year 5	$	1,891,171
Year 6	$	1,942,232
Year 7	$	1,994,672
Year 8	$	2,048,529
Year 9	$	2,103,839
Year 10	$	2,160,642
Year 11	$	2,218,980
Year 12	$	2,278,892
Year 13	$	2,340,422
Year 14	$	2,403,614
Year 15	$	2,468,511

This spreadsheet is available for free as a working Excel spreadsheet at Backofthenapkin.biz. You can customize it to analyze any rent vs. own analysis. I wanted to show you the full spreadsheet to give you a sense of the layout. For the sake of being able to actually read it, I have broken it into 2 pieces, namely the rent side and the own side. Let's take a look first at the rent side of this particular transaction.

Back of the Napkin

Rent vs. Own

123 Main Street, Anywhere USA

Building Size (square ft.)		13,500	Rent per Ft.	$ 21.00
Owner-User Space		3,670		
Additional Tenant Income		196,260		

Lease				Rent per Ft.
	Annual		Rent per Ft.	After Tax Deduction
Year 1	$	77,070	21.00	14.70
Year 2	$	80,153	21.84	15.29
Year 3	$	83,359	22.71	15.90
Year 4	$	86,693	23.62	16.54
Year 5	$	90,161	24.57	17.20
Year 6	$	93,767	25.55	17.88
Year 7	$	97,518	26.57	18.60
Year 8	$	101,419	27.63	19.34
Year 9	$	105,476	28.74	20.12
Year 10	$	109,695	29.89	20.92
Year 11	$	114,082	31.09	21.76
Year 12	$	118,646	32.33	22.63
Year 13	$	123,392	33.62	23.54
Year 14	$	128,327	34.97	24.48
Year 15	$	133,460	36.37	25.46

Total Rent Paid	$	1,543,218		$ 1,080,253

Average Cost per Foot after tax deduction based on 30% tax bracket			$ 19.62

Value at end of Lease	0	
Equity after 15 years	0	

44

The left half of the spreadsheet shows the rental analysis of this transaction. It shows the rent per foot of $21.00, the size of the space the owner/user is going to occupy-3,670 square feet and the total size of the building-13,500 square feet. This lease has 4% annual increases in the rent, which is the mid-range of 3-5% annual increases in this market. It shows the gross rental payments made over the 15-year life of the lease-$1,543,218. Since rent is an operating expense, it is tax deductible, so we show the net cost of rental assuming a 30% tax bracket. Needless to say, there is no equity and no value at the end of the lease period. We also see at the top of the spreadsheet the additional rental income of $196,260 which is annual rental income from the other tenants in the building. This will be needed when we look at the own side of the spreadsheet.

Now we will examine the own side of the spreadsheet, which is far more involved:

For starters, we see the purchase price, down payment, mortgage amount and annual debt service. Next, we have a breakdown of the operating expenses. The total annual carry, including debt service and expenses is $220,753. We then bring this down to a per-square-foot number by dividing the expenses into the building size. We see the per-square-foot carry cost is $16.35. We then calculate our

Own				Value Schedule		
Purchase Price	$	1,700,000		Based on Moodys and Real Capital Analytics. Historic		
Down Payment	$	900,000		Shows 14 year average increase in value of **5.4%**		
Mortgage	$	800,000		This model assumes <u>**half**</u> of the		
Annual Debt Service	$	61,853	25 year amort @6%	actual historical increase-2.7%		
Utilities	$	42,000				
Taxes	$	70,923		Year 1	$	1,700,000
Insurance	$	6,243		Year 2	$	1,745,900
Managem‹	$	14,274		Year 3	$	1,793,039
Janitorial	$	15,460		Year 4	$	1,841,451
Other Expenses	$	10,000		Year 5	$	1,891,171
Annual Carry Total	$	220,753		Year 6	$	1,942,232
Annual Carry per ft.		16.35		Year 7	$	1,994,672
				Year 8	$	2,048,529
				Year 9	$	2,103,839
				Year 10	$	2,160,642
Less Depreciation	$	34,871.79		Year 11	$	2,218,980
Effective Reduction	$	24,410	based on 30%	Year 12	$	2,278,892
Savings per Foot	$	1.81	tax bracket	Year 13	$	2,340,422
				Year 14	$	2,403,614
	$	16.35		Year 15	$	2,468,511
Net Depreciation	$	1.81				
Additional Tenant Inc.	$	14.53				
Effective Carry						
Per Foot	$	0.01	Sale in Yr. 15		$	2,468,511
			Mortgage balance yr. 15		$	464,275
			Net Equity after 15 years		**$**	**2,004,236**

depreciation, as this is treated like any other operating expense. We will dive into this in detail later in the book. Suffice it to say we take 80% of the purchase price and divide that by 39 to get our annual depreciation amount. 39 years is what the IRS code provides for real estate depreciation. As I said, depreciation is an expense that gets deducted from income like any other expense. Assuming a 30% tax bracket, the net effect of this deduction is a savings of $1.81 per square foot. This gets subtracted from the carry cost of $13.24. At this point, we apply the additional income from other tenants in the building of $196,260. We break this down to a per-square-foot basis by dividing the $196,260 by 13,500 square feet. This gives us an additional income of $14.53 per square foot. When we subtract this from the per-square-foot carry cost, we see that the other tenant's income actually offsets all of the expenses of the building. The bottom line here is that the owner/user of the building is in the space rent-free. As I said earlier, every deal will be different. Some deals will end up with partial supplementation of the expenses, and some, as in this case, result in a full offset of rental and actually have some positive cash flow on top of that. Don't forget the buyer needed to invest $900,000 to make this happen. For a buyer with $900,000, you may say this is a no-brainer. As I also said earlier, one must weigh the transaction very carefully. Let's suppose for a second that the potential buyer, in this case, could use the money to purchase raw materials for his widget business, which would produce a potential return of 25%. He may be better suited doing that. Possibly not an easy decision after all. Deploying capital is a very tricky process and all aspects have to be explored.

I need to give special recognition to my Back of the Napkin colleague, Ron Epstein, who helped me articulate this section in the way I envisioned it.

Back of The Napkin Summary Owner/User Properties

As illustrated, the owner/user analysis differs from an investor analysis. The starting point should be to analyze the property as an investment property to establish a "baseline" of value range. Ultimately, one would always want to know what a property is worth at arm's length based on investment criteria. That said, the owner/user has the "luxury" to go outside the box based on the fact that the property may potentially generate significant income from the business being placed there. If the owner/user determines he is willing to pay a premium for getting that location, at least it is being done with eyes wide open in respect to the actual value as an investment property. The owner/user analysis will also have a bit more in-depth analysis into items like local competition. If the intention is to open an Italian restaurant, it is imperative for the potential owner/user to research all the competition in the market. The owner/user needs to do the following:

1. Create a budget of all expenses and expenditures that will be spent creating the intended business. A reserve for operating expenses for the first year is also advisable. Many novice business owners make the mistake of assuming the revenue will

support the business once opened. Although a grand opening spike is common, once things settle down, you may find the income is not quite covering all of the expenses.

2. Research all competition for the intended business.

3. Research availability of all needed fixtures and equipment. As of the writing of this book, supply chain issues are still affecting the availability of many items needed to open a business. Unexpected downtime can be very costly.

4. REALISTICALLY pro-forma the first 3 years of revenue, preferably monthly if practical.

5. Research the different types of financing that may be available.

6. Obtain 1, 3, and 5 mile demographics showing population, income and community characteristics.

7. Obtain traffic counts to determine the actual level of car traffic. This is usually available from the state DOT website. If the location is very high foot traffic, then car counts may be unnecessary.

8. Analyze the benefits of renting versus owning if one has enough money for the down payment.

Back of The Napkin Checklist-Owner/User Properties

__Completed Rent Roll, if any tenants (form available at backofthenapkin.biz)

__Copy of all Leases and amendments, if any tenants

__Copy of Tax Bill(s)

__Survey, if available

__Detailed Income Expense Statement (form available at backofthenapkin.biz)

__Photos-Interior/exterior

__# of Parking Spaces

__# Lot size_____

__1, 3, and 5 mile demographics

__Traffic count (available from most DOT websites)

(answers in the back of the book)

1. As a potential owner/user property buyer, does a CAP rate analysis determine true value?

2. What are the typical mile radius demographics needed for an owner/user property?

3. What type of financing can owners/users qualify for?

4. Will an owner/user be willing to pay a premium for a property?

5. What percentage of a property has to be occupied by the owner to qualify for SBA financing?

6. What is a disadvantage to SBA financing?

7. Is traffic count relevant to an owner/user?

Back of The Napkin

Land/Land Development

At its most basic level, "Back of The Napkin" land analysis is fairly simple. The complicated part is getting there. Sounds confusing, I know, but we will get there. The value of land is determined by what you can do with it. If you have a 5-acre parcel that is mostly wetlands and therefore can't be developed, the commercial value is 0 unless someone wants to put a chaise lounge on it and watch the sunset (or sunrise as the case may be.) If a 5-acre parcel is properly zoned, say for retail, and is capable of supporting 40,000 square feet of retail space, then the value is potentially significant. There are still many factors that can and will affect the project's viability, and we will explore those.

Let's assume the owner of this 5-acre parcel is asking $3,000,000. How do we know if the property is worth that amount? We will need to analyze what can be done with the parcel and project the cost of developing the land, and the potential income that can be derived from the project. Comparable sales may or may not be valid as even the same size parcel across the street may be worth significantly more or less depending on many factors. The fact that the piece across the street sold for $1,000,000 can be very misleading in determining the value of the $3,000,000 parcel. Here are a few of the factors that will determine the value and the potential difference in the value of the parcels.

1. What is the zoning of the 2 parcels? One may be zoned for commercial use and the other for residential use, for argument's sake.

2. What is the topography of the 2 pieces? One may be flat as a pancake, the other very hilly. This can impact the cost of site work significantly.

3. How is the access to each piece? Is there a traffic light in front of one of them? Is one of the pieces on a corner?

4. What is the road frontage of the 2 pieces? One may have 50 feet of frontage and the other 500 feet of frontage. This will greatly impact the visibility of the project and how it will be constructed. Road frontage is critical, especially to retail, as road visibility of the center is paramount. Many smaller centers end up being built perpendicular to the road, which is far from ideal,

as there is little or no visibility of the actual tenants.

The most important factor that will determine the potential value is, you hopefully guessed it, the income that the project can generate. Only then can you determine whether the site is worth the asking price. Let's assume the project will be 40,000 square feet when completed. This is a reasonable approximate yield for a 5-acre site as rule of thumb, or the Back of the Napkin, says 20% yield on a site is usually reasonable, depending on many of the factors described above. Let's also assume an average rental of $25.00 per square foot net of all expenses. This means the tenants will pay the real estate taxes, the costs of maintaining the common areas, and possibly even the owner's property insurance premiums. This would mean that the income of $1,000,000 would basically be the net operating income (NOI). Based on a CAP Rate of 7%, this would establish the completed value at $14,285,714 ($1,000,000/.07).

As I said at the beginning, the Back of The Napkin analysis is fairly simple and will look like this:

Income generated by the project when complete: $1,000,000

Value of project when completed: (7 CAP) $14,000,000 (rounded)

Cost to develop: 40,000sf X $200 psf

$8,000,000 (this number is for illustration purposes only; an actual construction budget would need to be created, which is very detailed)

Potential profit:

$6,000,000

This means that after completion and tenants begin paying rent, there will be approximately $6,000,000 in equity value in the project. Depending on the profit margin a developer is working on, it becomes apparent that the project can support the $3,000,000 price tag for the land. Profit levels are an individual calculation and will vary greatly depending on the developer's motivations for a particular project.

As I also said, the complicated part is getting there. We will spend a good amount of time discussing this. When you follow "It's All in The Setup" the heavy lifting is done upfront, so the rest becomes easy.

From my perspective, land development is the ultimate real estate challenge. It also lends itself to the highest degree of creativity. A vacant parcel is a blank sheet of paper. Within the framework of zoning and good business practice, you can create a true masterpiece and make it profitable as well. This freedom also makes the process more complicated as you don't have a set "script" to follow. When I teach land use and development, I use the analogy of a developer being similar to a symphony orchestra conductor. The conductor must coordinate the strings, percussion, and horns, to name a few. They all need to work together to create the beautiful music. A developer must coordinate architects, engineers, attorneys, accountants, banks, brokers, tenants, and a host of others in order for the project to be successful. The process of ground-up development is extremely difficult in today's world. It is also expensive in terms of cash layout with no guarantee of success. In order to get all the zoning and municipal approvals needed, one needs to have legal help, engineering services, and architectural services, to name a few. There is no guarantee that after all is said and done, the project could be scaled back significantly from the original vision or worse, not approved at all.

The "Holy Grail" of land development is "Highest and Best Use." If fate is with the developer, then the highest and best use can be consistent with the parcel's zoning. If the zoning is inconsistent with the highest and best use, the developer may seek a zoning change. This process takes significant time, likely years, and has no guarantee of success. It is also expensive as a zoning attorney is required, as well as engineers and architects, to do preliminary plans. The process will also involve significant environmental reviews and studies. Suffice it to say a properly zoned piece is far more desirable. Even in that situation, the hoops that need to be jumped through are time-consuming and costly. The eventual positive outcome, although still not guaranteed, is far more likely.

The "Holy Grail" in land is the Highest and Best Use, which is determined by studying the market to determine what is actually needed. If the area has a shortage of office space, for example, then it makes sense to look in that direction. Through my affiliation as president of Polimeni International, LLC, I was involved with a 30-acre parcel on Veterans Highway in Islandia, NY. The property was zoned office/industrial. The property was a stone's throw from the Long Island Expressway, with over 200,000 cars per day passing by the site. Further, the area had an abundance of office space and the location with ample frontage on Veterans Highway was too good to be used for industrial, which at the time had significantly lower yields on value than either office or, in this case, retail. There was only one other shopping center in the market about 2 miles away. The rest of the corridor was office buildings and industrial. We did a market study and commissioned a survey of local residents to see what they would like. Vincent Polimeni, the primary principal of our company, took the approach very wisely that if the residents don't want a particular project it does not make sense to try to force it through. In this case, the survey showed that a shopping center was the second most desirable use of the land according to the residents. The most popular response was a park, which was not about to happen unless the village was willing to pay an enormous sum of money, which they were not. The market study also showed that a shopping center was the highest and best use of the land. This was based on the market's lower-than-average amount of retail square footage. The decision was made to attempt a full rezoning of the site. The process took 5 years and enormous legal and engineering bills; even when you think you are done, it is not always the case. On the night we got final approval from the Village of Islandia, we were approached by a Newsday reporter who asked us how we were going to deal with the "400-foot rule"? We all had that "deer in the headlights" expression on our faces when the question was asked. I don't remember the specifics of the rule, but the bottom line was that because of it we needed to get approvals from the town of Islip as well. The meeting ended around 10 pm, and our attorney went racing back to his office to read the town charter to verify this. He stayed in his office until midnight and, in fact, verified the reporter was correct. No matter how many bases you think are covered, there can always be one that gets missed. We had to go through much of the same process with Islip as we did with Islandia. We also got subsequent approval from the town of Islip, although it added more time and expense to the process.

The planning and approval process is time-consuming and arduous. This will involve the engineers and architects. Consideration needs to be given to sewage disposal, as this is critical if there are no sewers at the site. In our case, we needed to build a sewage treatment plant (STP) on site. This takes up space, which could potentially reduce yield and is very costly. Every town has "green area requirements." You can't just pave the entire site and build on every inch. In addition to everything else, a landscape plan must be submitted and approved as part of the site plan approval process. If you are on a state road, the state road department gets involved with the placement of curb cuts, distance of those cuts to traffic lights and the number of curb cuts. The board of health gets involved, you need input and approvals from the utility services, and the list goes on and on. The process will take time and cost significant dollars with no guarantee of final approvals. After all was said and done, the shopping center opened about 2 years later virtually fully leased.

Around the turn of the century, I actually got involved in development in Poland. My brother Alan had a colleague that owned a parcel of land near the German border. Our company was at a place in time where we were looking for a new challenge. This turned out to be a challenge with a capital C! Vincent Polimeni and I flew over and were completely blown away by what we found. The site was not appropriate for a typical shopping center, but the country was ripe for development. The per-capita square footage of retail space was about $1/10^{th}$ of that in the United States. Our initial vision was to bring American retailers like the Gap, and TJ Maxx to Poland. We found out quickly that was not to be. Its one thing to try to get these companies to Europe first. None of them were willing to make the leap from the U.S. to Poland. There were plenty of European retailers that did the same things as their U.S. counterparts. What we did find was a highly receptive country that actually wanted development. This was a breath of fresh air compared to the U.S. This project required basically relearning the real estate business from scratch. Land is not measured in acres there, instead, hectares, which is approximately 2.4 acres. No square footage either, square meters instead. And currency, well there's a doozy! The Polish currency was the Zloty, but lease payments were based on the Euro in most cases. The exchange rate calculations were enough to make you dizzy. Because of the harsh winters we decided to develop enclosed malls, instead of strip centers. Centrum Handlowe, as they are called were first coming into existence in the country, other than the big cities like

Warsaw, which had an abundance of retail. The development process was complicated as the country had just exited the red tape bureaucracy of communism. As long as you jumped through all the hoops you eventually got the permits. Financing in the beginning was also a challenge. Polish banks were lending based on 10-year self-liquidating loans. That was certainly not going to fly. As you know from prior lessons the debt service would wipe out all the cash flow, and then some. Fortunately, there were European banks that were in line with U.S. type financing. Our first center was in a city called Konin. We were basically the only shopping center in the city at the time. The only retail was scattered mom and pop stores. People wore ties and jackets to the grand opening. That's how much of an event this was. This is the link to the shopping center website, if you are curious: https://chgalerianadjeziorem.pl/sklepy/. We spent about 10 years and developed and sold 6 malls. Being a conductor on this stage was truly a challenge. Language barriers and customs differences helped make this an exciting, but ultimately rewarding experience. This could be a book in and of itself!

Back of The Napkin Summary-Land

The "Holy Grail" for land is the highest and best use. Further, land development, to me, is the "Holy Grail" of commercial real estate. It is the most complicated, risky, and challenging of any persuasion of commercial real estate. It also allows for the highest degree of creativity and profit. Zoning and the possible need for zone change are important to consider. You will need a large team of professionals and deep pockets or partners willing to fund to pay for this with no guarantee of a successful outcome. The main professionals needed will be an attorney, especially one expert in zoning matters, a great broker to help with pre-leasing, an architect, an engineer, and a bank, to name a few.

Back of The Napkin Checklist-Land

__Survey

__Zoning

__Topographical Map. If available

__Copy of Tax Bill(s)

__Aerial photo

__Detailed Income Expense Statement (form available at backofthenapkin.biz)

__1, 3 1nd 5 mile demographics

__Traffic count (available from most DOT websites)

(answers in the back of the book)

1. How is the highest and best use determined?

2. What is a topographical map?

3. Why is road frontage important to a retail project?

4. What is the most important factor that affects the value of land?

5. List 3 professionals that developers need to coordinate.

Back of The Napkin-

The Purchase Process

Regardless of property type, the purchase process is very similar. There are nuances based on whether a property is multi-family, retail, industrial, office or land, but the process is still the same. In subsequent chapters we will provide the information and detail you need regarding all property types.

All transactions will begin with a negotiating process, which involves the purchaser making an offer. Unless you are an experienced real estate owner, I strongly recommend the use of a quality commercial real estate broker. With my 40+ years of experience, I, as a seller, will not sell a property I own without the use of a broker. In fact, I hired the previously mentioned Ron Epstein as my broker when I sold 2 properties I owned on Long Island. Both were successfully sold. The old expression "a lawyer who represents himself has a fool for a client" applies here, in my view. A quality broker will not only know the ins and outs of transaction structure, but they will also have local market expertise to guide you on things like local market rents, comparable sales, and things going on in the market that may impact the property you are looking to buy or sell and many other details too numerous to mention. If you are purchasing, then I strongly also recommend aligning yourself with a good local attorney to get you through the transaction. If you are purchasing a property in a suburban county, I would not advise using a city lawyer. They just won't have the local knowledge you will require. Further, as an owner, emotion can get in the way. Especially during the negotiating process, I have witnessed owners/sellers becoming their own worst enemies. A good broker is going to listen to both sides and strip out the "noise" in order to keep the negotiation objective and on track.

Any offer should be in writing and be as complete as possible. Putting it in writing lends credibility to the offer and ensures all items are included in the initial offer as well as any subsequent counteroffers, which will invariably occur. The offer should include the following items. A letter of intent form (as well as forms for numerous other items) is available for your use for free on backofhtenapkin.biz.

Property Address: You can't buy a property if you don't know where it is!

Parties: The purchaser or purchasing entity and the

seller or entity that owns the property should be stated.

Purchase Price: A buyer rarely offers the full asking price as most sellers price the property expecting some negotiation.

Contract Deposit: When the contracts are executed, there is typically a 5-10% deposit placed in escrow with (usually the seller's) attorney or with a title company, depending on which state the transaction is occurring.

Closing Date: Depending on the transaction type and size of the transaction, the amount of time to close (or settle) will vary. Closing dates can either be "on or about" which means the actual closing date is not cast in stone and customarily will allow for 30 days past the posted closing date in the contract, or "time is of the essence" which means the date is the date, which could become problematic. Time is of the essence means that the transaction MUST close on the date, or the party that does not show up for virtually any reason will be held in default. The type of closing date will vary state by state and local custom. As a purchaser, you are free to offer whatever structure you would like. Keep in mind the more time you request to close, the less likely a seller is to accept it.

Conditions Prior to Closing: This is a critical part of the offer as it spells out the purchaser's expectations and conditions necessary to close the transaction. Sometimes, there is what is known as a full "due diligence" period, which typically gives the purchaser full right to cancel the contract for any or no reason prior to the conclusion of the due diligence period. This type of due diligence period is more common in larger, more complex transactions that involve the review of numerous leases and extensive financial data. It is too expensive, between lawyers and accountants, to verify and read numerous documents prior to contract signing, and it also exposes the purchaser to the seller possibly taking a different deal. A due diligence period can range from 30 to 90 days, depending on the property type and complexity of the transaction. The time period is completely negotiable between the parties. Other conditions usually include an environmental review to see if there is any possibility of contaminants on the property. This process begins with a phase 1 review, which only involves reviewing the history of the property to see if any uses may have introduced contaminants to the site. Town records are reviewed as well, along with a visual inspection of the property and improvements. If the property was or is used for any industrial purpose other than warehousing, such as automotive use, or any use involving any type of toxic chemicals, the property may be subject to a phase 2 study where core samples of dirt are actually taken and analyzed. Should there be any issues, the purchaser would have the right to cancel the contract or the seller may be obligated to remediate up to a certain dollar amount. All transactions are also subject to a "clean" title, meaning there are no issues affecting the title of the property.

Mortgage Contingency: If the contract contains a due diligence period as described above, a mortgage contingency is not usually included or needed as the purchaser will be arranging the financing during this period. If unsuccessful, the purchaser has the unilateral right to cancel the contract and receive a refund of the contract deposit. If the contract does not contain this type of due diligence period, then it is possible to have a mortgage contingency if the parties agree. The mortgage contingency needs to contain the number of days the purchaser has to obtain a commitment and the amount of financing the purchaser is seeking. If either is unrealistic, then the seller will likely not agree to those terms.

Once these major terms are agreed to, it is helpful if a letter of intent (LOI) is executed by the parties. It is non-binding and subject to the execution of a formal contract, but it will serve as the basis for the seller's attorney to create the contract. The seller's attorney is typically the party that generates the sale contract.

Let's look at what a typical, basic LOI would look like for a transaction.

OFFER TO PURCHASE

Date: March 6, 2022

Re: **Letter of Intent to purchase the real property located at : 123 Any Street USA**

We are pleased to present this offer to purchase the above referenced property on behalf of the propo
purchaser. Please find proposed terms meant to outline the business arrangement that purchaser wou
willing to proceed forward with:

PURCHASE PRICE:

SELLER:

PURCHASER:

CONTRACT DEPOSIT: The initial deposit shall be $_____ to be held in escrow by se
attorney, upon execution of contract. The contract shall be subject to a 45-day Due Diligence Period

DUE DILIGENCE PERIOD: Commencing on execution of the contract to purchase the above
referenced property, the Purchaser shall have the right to review all leases, review all income and ex
records, have an engineer inspect the property, and have a phase 1 environmental study performed, a
with any other examination of the property that the Purchaser may deem necessary. Seller agrees to
furnish all leases and financial records to Purchaser, or his chosen designee, for review, and to coope
with Purchasers requests. On or before the 45th day the Purchaser shall have the right to cancel the
contract of sale for any, or no reason, and have the initial deposit returned in full. Should the purcha
decide to proceed with the purchase then the deposit shall be increased to 10% of the purchase price.
($_____). At that point, the deposit will become non-refundable, unless there is a title issue
can't be cured.

NO MORTGAGE CONTINGENCY: This transaction is not subject to financing, but Purchaser m
acquire financing. Seller agrees to cooperate with Purchasers lender, should there be one.

CLOSING DATE: On or about:

The above is not intended to be contractual in nature, or to set forth all of the relevant busin
terms and conditions that will be included in the sales contract, but is intended to be an
expression of the general business terms and conditions upon which buyer and seller are wil
to proceed with.

Regards,

_____ Date _____
Purchaser

_____ Date _____
Seller

Keep in mind this particular LOI is very basic and only includes the basic business terms of the transaction. I have seen very complex LOI's that almost resemble a contract of sale. Keeping in mind my Back of the Napkin mentality I do not subscribe to this way of thinking. Firstly, it becomes very time consuming and secondly some LOI's wade into lawyer territory, which can become problematic.

This transaction does not contain a mortgage contingency, as it is not necessary because purchaser has the right to cancel for any or no reason. If one is not experienced with this type of transaction, the counsel of a good commercial real estate broker, or attorney is advisable. Keep in mind this is not a binding contract, therefore a Broker can assist. Any binding agreement will be the purview of an attorney only, in many states.

Once the LOI is agreed to the Sellers attorney will prepare the contract of sale. The attorneys will usually dicker back and forth a bit to justify their fees and ultimately the contract will be executed by the parties, with a contract deposit posted. There are no hard and fast rules on deal structure. That said, certain things are normally done after contracts are signed and a deposit is posted. When we discuss financing in the next chapter, we will cover this. The purchaser then needs to complete all due diligence and line up the financing. It is always a good start to approach the bank that the purchaser has a relationship with. Past that there are many banks that will issue financing. Let's spend a few minutes on that topic. We will go in-depth in the financing chapter. Commercial real estate financing is far different than residential lending. Of course, there are always regional differences, but I will focus on the East Coast, U.S., as I am most familiar with that. Residential lending is very focused on the purchaser, with somewhat strict debt-to-income ratio limits and income verification as well. Of course, the property needs to be appraised as well. As you probably know, residential mortgages can be as long as 30 years self-liquidating, with numerous other iterations available as well, such as variable rate mortgages, interest-only mortgages, and even reverse mortgages where no payments are required. (age restrictions apply to reverse mortgages) Commercial real estate mortgages are more property-focused. The buyer still has to prove creditworthiness, but personal income is secondary to the income of the property in the case of investment property. Rates are usually pegged to the treasury bill, usually 5 years, plus a spread. Loan to value is usually around 70-75% of the appraised value. (The loan-to-value on SBA loans is significantly higher, and we will cover that shortly.) This can be a bit misleading as when a bank underwrites a commercial real estate mortgage, they include certain items that may not affect actual cash flow. Two examples are management fees and vacancy factors. Even if a property is self-managed by the owner, the bank will underwrite a management fee into the expenses as they make the assumption that if the property is foreclosed by the bank, a property manager will need to be hired. The same applies to the vacancy factor, even if the property is fully leased. The bank will usually deduct, say, 4-10% from the actual gross income to provide for the possible loss of tenant(s). These two items basically lower the actual loan to value, thereby resulting in less loan proceeds to the borrower. Commercial real estate loans also generally are much shorter term than residential mortgages, with most having a 10-year term with a rate reset after 5 years. No, don't expect that rate to decrease after 5 years, even if rates fall, as the loan will contain an interest floor. The purchaser could consider refinancing with another financial institution at that point but will have to weigh the potential interest savings against the cost of refinancing. Another consideration is that commercial real estate mortgages commonly have a prepayment penalty. A typical formula is 5-4-3-2-1, which is a 5% prepayment penalty in the first year, 4% in the second, and so on.

Back of The Napkin Summary-Purchase Process

The purchase process can be very complicated, especially for the novice investor. There is much to know and do to protect yourself and to analyze the property you are purchasing properly. If you are buying for investment, it's all about the return. You need to weigh the return against other types of investment, such as stocks, bonds and annuities, to name a few. Keep in mind that real estate is not a liquid investment. You can't call your broker and tell them to sell today like you can with liquid investments. It is very important to do your due diligence. Analyze all leases and financial data thoroughly. Use your professionals like lawyers and accountants. Yes, it will cost, but look at the price of getting it wrong.

I suggest using a qualified broker. I have been doing commercial real estate for over 40 years. I have not sold any of my properties without the use of a broker, although I am very qualified to do so.

Document everything from the letter of intent. Make sure you insist on all pre-closing conditions you need.

If you are buying as a user, then your outlook will be very different. You still will need to complete due diligence for all items necessary, but your financial analysis will be significantly different. You will look at the property through the eyes of a business owner, trying to calculate the amount of revenue your business will generate at this location. You may be able to justify a higher price than an investor.

Back of The Napkin-Purchase Process-Checklist

Investor

__Completed Rent Roll, if any tenants (form available at backofthenapkin.biz)

__Copy of all Leases and amendments, if any tenants

__Copy of Tax Bill(s)

__Survey, if available

__Detailed Income Expense Statement (form available at backofthenapkin.biz)

__Photos-Interior/exterior

__# of Parking Spaces

__# Lot size_____

__Letter of intent

__Attorney and Accountant

__Potential Lenders (unless all cash)

Owner User-in addition to above

__1, 3- and 5-mile demographics

__Traffic count (available from most DOT websites)

__Competition survey

Back of The Napkin-Purchase Process-Review

(answers in the back of the book)

1. What are the 2 most important professionals needed in a purchase of commercial property?

2. When should an offer not be in writing?

3. What is a mortgage contingency?

4. In general, can bank financing be procured without a phase 1 environmental review?

5. List 3 things a purchaser needs to do during the due diligence period.

6. Why is 'time is of the essence" bad?

Back of the Napkin-Financing

(Acknowledgment to Mac Wilcox, President of Hanover Bank, for his assistance in this section)

The financing process is complicated as well. This section is not intended to earn you a degree in financing but instead provide an overview at 30,000 feet to give you insights as to how financing works in the commercial world and the different types of financing available. In addition to my experience of over 40 years in commercial real estate, I also serve on the Board of Directors of Hanover Bank, headquartered in Mineola, N.Y., and have done so since its inception in 2008. Additionally, I am Chairperson of the credit committee, which approves loans over certain thresholds. In that capacity, I have reviewed thousands of loans over the years. Financing commercial real estate is very different than financing a house purchase. In the residential world, as you probably know, there is an abundance of 15 or 30-year fixed or variable-rate mortgages. These mortgages are usually sold off in the secondary markets as banks don't want to take interest rate risk for up to 30 years. Again, keep in mind that residential real estate includes single-family homes, co-ops, condominiums and multifamily up to 4-family properties. 5 families and up is considered commercial real estate from a financial perspective.

The first significant difference is the loan term. Investment commercial real estate loans typically have 5- or 10-year terms, with amortization of anywhere from 20-30 years. Interest rates typically reset after 5 years unless loans are floating rate, meaning the rate adjusts periodically based on the prime rate or treasury bills, for example. Banks add a spread to these indexes, creating the actual rates you will pay. Depending on the purchase price you will have several options to obtain financing. Most banks will offer up to 75% financing based on loan-to-value. This does not mean 75% of the purchase price, as the property will be appraised at the borrower's expense. If the appraisal is lower than the contract price, the loan will be based on 75% of the appraised value. If the property appraises above the contract price, then the loan will be based on the contract price. Oh, and by the way, if that happens, congrats, you likely bought the property right! Going further, the 75% might not actually be 75%. What do I mean by that? Let's assume the current owner is self-managing the property and not taking a management fee. The Bank is going to underwrite the loan, taking into account a reasonable management fee, say 3-5% of the gross income. This will have the effect of lowering the income of the property, even though currently, no management fee is being paid. Adding insult to injury, the bank will likely underwrite the loan, accounting for a vacancy factor. Even if the property is fully leased, the bank will deduct up to 10% assuming a tenant or tenants are lost. The net effect of all of this is to reduce the actual loan value to as low as 65% or so. The bank will also look at the debt service coverage ratio, or DSCR, to ensure there will be cash flow of at least 120% of the debt. DSCR is calculated by dividing the net operating income by the total debt service inclusive of principal and interest.

In most cases, personal guarantees will be required as personal net worth and credit scores become more important.

I always recommend starting your search with the bank you do the most business with. Relationships do matter, especially if you bank with a smaller local or regional bank. Keep in mind from a bank's perspective it's all about the deposit relationship. Banks need deposits to be able to keep making loans. The more you can keep on deposit, the more interested they will be in lending to you. Keep in mind virtually all commercial real estate loans have what is known as a pre-payment penalty. This means if you pay off the loan prior to its maturity, you will pay a penalty. This will vary from bank to bank, but a typical prepayment penalty for a loan with a 5-year term and a 5-year renewal option might have a 5% penalty in the first year, 4% the second and a declining penalty to 1% in the final year. Most loans will provide a window of no penalty if paid off in the loan's last "X" months. If the loan is extended, the prepayment penalty will reset.

If you bank with a larger bank, say, Chase or B of A, for example, you may find they have higher minimum loan amounts. This will vary regionally and by property type.

If you plan on buying a property for your business to use, you may qualify for what is known as SBA financing. SBA stands for Small Business Administration. You can qualify if you will occupy 51% or more of the property. The advantage of SBA financing is a lower down payment. This will vary depending on loan type. There is an array of SBA loans, such as microloans of up to $50,000, for use to reopen or rebuild a business. The larger maximum loans of up to $5.5 million can be used to acquire owner/user real estate, as well as leasehold improvements and equipment. The disadvantage to SBA financing is that it is more expensive with fees and a higher interest rate. If you intend to buy property for your own use it would behoove to research this option. Two primary types of SBA loans are the 7A and 504 programs. The 7A program allows more flexibility as the funds can be used for working capital and equipment acquisition, to name a few. The 504 program is primarily designed for real estate acquisition. Should you have any questions about any SBA financing, I invite you to call Elijiah Gray, First Senior Vice President, Hanover Bank-212-277-4358, and she will be happy to answer any questions you have.

Financing begins with the lender usually issuing a term sheet. This is exactly what it implies. It spells out the terms on which the bank may issue a loan. The term sheet is NOT a commitment. The term sheet will outline all the terms of the potential loan, such as amount, loan term, and interest rate structure, to list a few. The term sheet will also list conditions for approval. The bank will need all leases, if any, all financial information on the property and your personal financial information. Unlike residential loans, commercial loans are not tied to a hard and fast calculation of your income-to-debt ratio. The bank will want a comfort level regarding your financial status and a verification of assets to be used to close the loan. The major focus on an investment property loan will be the property itself. Income and expense verification will be paramount. A thorough review of all leases will occur as well. Lease term is a significant factor in underwriting the loan. If a property has only short-term leases, the lender is going to be concerned about loss of cash flow when those leases expire. It is fine to have some short-term leases depending on how many tenants are in the property. Terms of 5 years or more certainly make the lender more comfortable. Tenant quality is also important. How long has the tenant been in business? Is the tenant creditworthy? In other words, if you have Joe's Coffee Shop as opposed to Starbucks, the lender is not going to be as comfortable with Joe's. Do any of the leases have early termination clauses? That type of clause gives the tenant the right to terminate the lease under certain conditions before the expiration date. We will discuss this type of clause in detail in the leasing section. Suffice it to say, the lender, rightly so, will be concerned with many details of the leases in the property.

Financing commercial real estate is not inexpensive. The borrower is responsible for items such as an appraisal, which can cost $2-3,000 or more depending on property size and type, bank attorney fees, which will vary, and what is known as a phase 1 environmental review. This can also cost north of $2,000. This review is important as the bank (and you) want to make sure the property is not contaminated. A phase 1 review looks at the history of the property and its past uses, as well as current tenants. The reviewer will also check town records to see if anything indicates a potential environmental issue. If anything indicates a potential contamination, then a phase 2 study will be needed. This includes test borings of the soil to test for contamination. If the property currently has a dry cleaner other than a drop store, this will be a major red flag, as those chemicals frequently work their way into the soil. A huge red flag is a gas station, as they have historically been responsible for much contamination. If an underground gas tank leaks, it can cause what is known as a plume under neighboring properties. The cost of remediation can be millions. Suffice it to say it is imperative to verify the environmental condition of the property prior to closing. Physical inspection of the building, its roof, structural soundness, parking lot(s) and mechanicals, such as HVAC units (heat and air conditioning), is also important and will cost anywhere from $1,000 up depending on the size and type of the property.

Once everything is verified, a commitment is issued. This is what it implies, namely, a commitment to make the loan, possibly still subject to certain other conditions. All loans are subject to a "clean" title. This ensures there are no violations or liens other than those put in place by the current owner, such as the current mortgage. Once all conditions in the commitment have been fulfilled, a closing would be the next stop.

As with any other service, it pays to shop your loan with several lenders. One option is to use a mortgage broker. The plus to this is the fact a truly experienced mortgage broker will know exactly which lenders will look at your loan, and they can shop it to several sources at once. The borrower typically pays a fee of, say, 1% of the loan, depending on the loan size. The larger the loan, the more leverage the borrower will have to negotiate the fee. It may be worthwhile to pay this fee as you could potentially save thousands over the life of the loan if the broker finds a loan with a competitive rate.

A quick word about other types of loans in the commercial real estate world. Back in the 1980s, securitized loans, or CMBS (Commercial Mortgage-Backed Securities), emerged and were very popular. The concept was quite ingenious as loans were pooled into very large pools, say billions of dollars. They were split into tranches or sliced. They were then sold on Wall Street, with the lowest-risk tranches being sold at premiums and the highest-risk tranches sold for less, thus yielding a higher return. In 2008, the financial crisis hit, and CMBS fell out of favor. These loans allowed for up to 80% LTV and lower interest rates and mostly apply to larger loans. They are now back in favor, albeit with more conservative underwriting and safeguards.

Life insurance companies also play a role in commercial real estate financing. They typically finance class-A properties and offer advantages such as competitive interest rates and longer-term self-liquidating mortgages.

Financing land purchases is a bit more challenging. Based on the obvious reason of lack of any cash flow, this poses a risk for the lender. There is SBA financing for land, and a limited number of banks will also provide land financing under certain conditions. Seller financing is viable and possibly advantageous for the seller as well. Let's say a piece of land sells for $2,000,000. The seller likely would want 50% down and to hold a mortgage for the other $1,000,000. The seller could likely achieve a better rate of return on the mortgage than he could, depositing the funds in a bank. If I were the seller, I would want 7 or 8%. The land secures the loan, so worst case, the seller keeps the $1,000,000 down payment and gets to sell the land again. Further, capital gains taxes are paid as the seller receives the mortgage payments, creating the opportunity to defer taxes. This seller financing option is valid for any commercial property. Eventually, if it's a land sale, the new owner will create a plan for developing the property, at which point he can apply for construction financing. Construction financing also poses a risk for a bank as there is still no cash flow. The bank will likely insist on a certain level of pre-leasing, except in the case of multi-family projects, before disbursing funds. In a commercial project, say retail, tenants are willing to wait for construction to be complete.

Back of The Napkin Summary-Financing

Financing is complicated, with many steps and a ton of paperwork. Refer back to "It's all in the Setup". Take a deep breath and tackle each piece one at a time. The same way you would eat an elephant—one bite at a time.

Make sure you conduct thorough due diligence. Use an accountant and an attorney. I know it costs money, but how about avoiding a potentially multi-million-dollar mistake? Leases are complicated and may contain certain provisions that create problems for the landlord. There could be early termination rights or clauses obligating the landlord to certain costs that you should at least know about prior to buying a property. The financial information provided needs to be verified. Mistakes in those numbers could alter the value significantly. Any misrepresentation of expenses is something that could haunt you after the closing.

Start with your current bank and see what they say. If the loan is not for them, you may consider hiring a mortgage broker. Determine what type of financing is best for your transaction. Conventional, SBA, maybe even seller financing. Make sure there is enough time in your contract to complete financing. Even if your transaction is not subject to financing, you won't be able to get to the closing table in, say, 30 days. Allow 90-120 days and try to avoid "time is of the essence" closing requirements. On or about gives you more flexibility. Make sure your attorney reviews your term sheet. Rule of thumb-if you are going to sign something, anything, have it reviewed by a competent attorney. Accept the fact that commercial financing is expensive. Third-party reports, bank attorney, your attorney, origination fees, to name a few.

If you are an owner/user, explore SBA loans. They afford a lower downpayment and money for leasehold improvements and equipment. They are more expensive, but keep in mind, you may be able to deploy your capital for a higher return than the cost of the loan.

All in all, organization and thoroughness are key. If it turns out this transaction is not for you, lick your wounds and go on to the next one.

Back of The Napkin Checklist-Financing

__Hire an attorney.

__Hire an accountant.

__List of potential lenders and/or mortgage brokers.

__Copy of all leases.

__All financial information for at least the current and prior year.

__Assessment of the best type of loan for your transaction.

(answers in the back of the book)

1. What do banks analyze to determine if the is enough cash flow to support a loan?

2. What is the SBA 504 program primarily for?

3. What is the document issued when a loan has been approved by the bank?

4. What is a prepayment penalty?

5. What is the advantage of a mortgage broker?

6. What occurs in a phase 2 environmental review?

7. Are SBA loans more or less expensive than conventional financing?

8. What does CMBS stand for?

9. What is the advantage of CMBS financing?

10. What will a lender "likely" require in construction project financing?

Back of the Napkin-Tax Ramifications

(Acknowledgment to Gary Sanders, CPA, for his assistance in this section)

Buying and selling commercial real estate has short- and long-term tax consequences. There are methods to defer taxes as well, which we will discuss. If you purchase an investment property, you should consider holding it for more than one year. If you sell it prior to that time, the tax on any gain will be higher than if you hold it for a longer period of time. Considering all the costs and efforts of purchasing commercial property, I do not recommend looking at this as a short-term investment. Furthermore, it is highly unlikely you will have a significant enough gain in a short period of time, as values are tied to income growth, and unless there is some extenuating circumstance, it is not likely you would see a big enough gain to make it worth the expense.

The first tax ramification we will talk about is

depreciation. What is depreciation? It is defined as a "loss of value". If you buy, say, factory equipment, the day you buy that equipment, it will have lost some value. It's the same as when you buy a car. It goes down in value every year. In the business world the tax code allows a business to take that depreciation as an expense, thus reducing the taxable income of that business. In those situations, depreciation actually makes sense as the value is truly going down. However, the government also allows us to depreciate investment real estate. My guess is half of Congress back in the day owned commercial property, so they wanted that tax break. Unlike cars and factory equipment, investment real estate usually appreciates over time, so there really is no "loss of value" as is the case with equipment and the like. Commercial property can be depreciated on a "straight line" basis over 39 years. Keep in mind that the cost allocated to the building and the improvements on the land can be depreciated. Although the actual cost attributable to land is not depreciated, any improvements to the land can indeed be depreciated over their useful life. Examples of these improvements would be paving a driveway, fencing, or outdoor lighting. The government wasn't stupid enough to say that the land itself would lose value. You can use the property tax assessor's values to compute the ratios of a purchase price attributable to land vs building or any other reasonable estimate. Many times, an allocation of 80% towards the building and 20% to land is deemed to be acceptable, although it would vary based on circumstances. As an example, if you purchase a piece of property for $1,000,000, you would consider attributing 80% or $800,000 toward the building and $200,000 is attributed toward the land. It is arbitrary, but it does pretty much work. If you depreciate $800,000 over a 39-year period, this will create an expense of $20,512 dollars per year. This amount gets deducted from operating income as if you had written a check for it. This will have the effect of reducing your taxable income by $20,512.

While discussing Depreciation, the concept of "cost segregation" should be briefly discussed. Often, when making a purchase, there are various structural components that can be depreciated based on their shorter lifespan and possibly even more accelerated methods. This would also apply to the identification of improvements made during the course of ownership. If a cost segregation study is undertaken by hiring a professional or conducting your own study, then perhaps certain structural components can be depreciated under much shorter and more accelerated methods. Examples would be flooring, windows, or elevators.

Speaking of other faster depreciation deductions, let's

not ignore the cost of structural improvements to the interior of the building or, under recent laws, the cost of roofs or heating/air-conditioning units, called "qualified improvement property (QIP)." The QIP asset class first came into the tax code as part of a 2015 law that created it for property placed in service on or after Jan. 1, 2016. It was defined as "any improvement to an interior portion of a building which is nonresidential real property if such improvement is placed in service after the date such building was first placed in service." Certain types of improvements were specifically excluded from QIP, such as the enlargement of the building, any elevator or escalator, or the changes to the internal structural framework of the building.

These improvements can be expensed under bonus depreciation at different percentages based on dates placed in service and the rates allowed for immediate deduction for that year.

The bonus depreciation, or the amount over what would have been a straight line allowed, is subject to ordinary income rates at the time of sale.

Let's take a quick look at land lease scenarios. With a land lease, the property owner does not own the land under the building. Instead, there are rental payments made for the "use" of the land. Let's use the same example as before, where the property is purchased for $1,000,000. Since the land is not part of the transaction, the purchaser can depreciate the full $1,000,000, creating a depreciation expense of $25,641 per year. Further, the ground rent is an expense and as such, tax deductible. The negative in this scenario is that you don't have control over the underlying land, which could eventually become problematic.

Be aware that when you sell the property, there is what is called depreciation recapture. In essence, you have gotten an interest-free loan for the time that you owned the property.

The Depreciation recapture would lower the actual cost of the property for tax purposes and, in effect, increase the profit upon sale.

Another popular technique is to negotiate a sale where the seller holds a mortgage secured by the property with market interest being paid and future principal payments. This provides the seller with an opportunity to receive interest on the money while deferring taxes on the percentage of the profit being deferred until the principal is paid in future years. The only caveat is that the ratio of profit resulting from depreciation recapture can't be deferred, which means care must be taken to assure enough of a downpayment to cover taxes due in the year of the sale.

There is a way to defer that depreciation recapture and other profit through what is known as a 1031-like kind exchange. In this scenario, the seller of the property sells an investment property with the intent of purchasing another piece of property. The seller has 45 days to identify the replacement property, which must be the same or higher value. If there is a mortgage on the property being sold, then the replacement property must also have a mortgage of equal or higher value. A "qualified intermediary"(QI), takes possession of the funds from the sale, so the seller never actually takes possession of the money. The new transaction must close within 180 days from the sale of the previous property. "Like kind' does not mean if you sell a shopping center, you must buy a shopping center. One can replace any type of investment or commercial real property in a 1031 exchange. This does not apply to a primary residence, which has completely different tax laws.

One final thought on completely eliminating any taxes on the appreciation or depreciation recapture is to simply own the property at the time of death and pass to heirs' income tax-free!

If you own the property at death, there is a "step-up" in basis to the market value on the date of your passing.

This basically erases any cost improvement expenditure and ignores any depreciation recapture.

Your heirs would receive a basis in the property equal to the fair market value on your day of death.

In many cases, if there are no estate taxes, as the decedent is below the filing threshold, waiting may be best, but extreme care and consideration to federal and state estate taxes must be examined carefully.

Back of the Napkin-Tax Ramifications-Review

(answers in the back of the book)

1. What is the number of years that real estate can be depreciated?

2. What is the definition of depreciation?

3. Can land be depreciated?

4. What is the advantage of a 1031 exchange?

5. What happens with depreciation when you sell a property and don't do a 1031 exchange?

6. How many days does a seller have to identify a replacement property in a 1031 exchange?

7. What is the advantage of a land lease?

8. What is a QI?

Back of The Napkin-Leases

In this section, we will discuss leases in general. I will then go on to discuss the different types of leases: office, retail and industrial. They all have their own nuances and are very different from each other, with the exception of industrial, which mostly contains all the standard clauses.

A lease, simply put, is a contract. It establishes a landlord-tenant relationship. Today's leases are quite complicated and certainly require the input of a qualified attorney to review and modify the lease. It is important to distinguish between business terms and legal issues. In my view, it is best not to let the attorney negotiate the business points. I feel that it is better left to the tenant with the aid of a qualified broker. There are actually brokers that not only specialize in leasing but further, the specific types of properties I just outlined. If you are looking to lease, say, retail space, you are best suited to research the best retail leasing brokers in your area. The same goes for office and industrial leases. A broker who specializes in the particular area you are considering will know what the fair market rents are, what typical rent increases are, they will know what typical solutions are for many of the business points.

As I stated, a lease is a contract. It is a contract that typically binds the parties for several years. Leases can typically run from 3-20 years or more and anything in between. It is possible to have a 1-year lease, but unless there is a specific reason, it is not the best solution for several reasons. For example, if you are going to open a business, it does not make much sense to spend significant dollars on leasehold improvements, inventory, and IT installations, which are very costly, just to be forced to move in 1or 2 years should the landlord not choose to renew your lease. In my view, 5 years plus at least one 5-year option is a better way to go. A one-year lease may be suitable for, say, a candidate who needs a field office while running for election. This is an example of a use with a finite time period. There are not many uses that fit that bill. If the concern is you may outgrow the space in less than 5 years, then it is possible to negotiate what is known as an early termination right. Landlords generally do not like this as it potentially shortens the potential time period the tenant would be in occupancy based on the lease term. For financing purposes, landlords and lenders generally like leases with longer terms, as discussed in the financing section. Simply put, an early termination clause is simply that. In my experience, it always has certain conditions attached. For example, the clause may say that after 3 years of a 5-year lease, the tenant may elect, in writing, to exercise the right to terminate. There may be a penalty of 3 or 6 months rent along with forfeiture of the security deposit. There are no hard and fast conditions for an early termination, as it is completely subject to negotiation. In most cases, a landlord will not agree to do this at all, especially if the particular space is in demand. If a space is sitting vacant for an extended period, a landlord would be more inclined to consider an early termination right in order to get the space leased.

Let's spend some time highlighting the clauses found in all types of leases. We will then discuss the clauses and nuances of each commercial space category, namely, retail, office and industrial.

Demised Premises-This describes the space that is to be leased by the tenant. It can be described by a suite number or some other identifier. The size will usually, but not always, be noted as well. Some landlords try to avoid specifying the size because if it turns out to be inaccurate, there could be an attempt to recover any possible overpayment of rent. If a landlord represents that a space is 1,000 square feet and the tenant is paying, say, $20 per square foot, totaling $20,000 per annum in rent, and the space turns out to be 950 square feet, the tenant may try to recover an overpayment of $1,000 per year times the number of years of the overpayment. A way to avoid this and still have the size of the space in the lease is the use of the following language: "which the parties agree is 1,000 square feet." This language indicates that both parties are in agreement on this fact, eliminating the possible litigation for overpayment of rent.

Base Term- This is the length of time the tenant is leasing the space. "The term of this lease shall be for a period of 5 years".

Lease Commencement- This is when the lease itself begins. This is typically upon occupancy of the space.

Rent Commencement- This is not necessarily the same as a Lease Commencement. There may be a rent concession for a period of months, which would have been negotiated prior. If there was a 60-day rent concession, rent would commence on day 61 of the term of the lease.

*Annual Increases-*How much the rent will go up and when. It could be an annual increase, which is typical, or any other schedule that the parties agree on.

*Utilities-*In one way or another, the Tenant will usually pay for utilities in a commercial lease. The space could have separate meters for electricity, gas or water. In the alternative, some leases provide for a flat per square foot charge, say $3.50 =$4.00 per foot, which is fairly typical for Long Island. There are other less common methods that we will ignore.

*Tax Increases-*This clause will vary based on property type which we will cover specifically in each property type. Suffice it to say there is usually some form of partial or full tax reimbursement in commercial leases. This is not always the case, though.

*Use-*If the space is office or industrial; the use does not need to be as specific as it does in a retail setting. When we discuss retail, we will go into detail, but suffice it to say that, especially in a shopping center setting, use is very important.

Option(s)- In addition to the base term there may be additional option(s) to renew based on whatever terms the parties agree.

*Security Deposit-*Virtually all leases, other than a "national" credit tenant, have a security deposit paid by the Tenant and held by the Landlord. In a commercial lease the Security need not be held in a separate account, unlike apartment leases.

*Landlord Work-*Spells out what improvements, if any, that the landlord is responsible for prior to Tenant taking possession. This is usually very detailed and specific, so there is no misunderstanding by either party. Many times the space will be turned over "as is", meaning Landlord has no responsibility for improvements.

Tenant Work-If the Tenant will be performing work in the Demised Premises, this will stipulate things like during what hours they can perform work and will specify that the work be done by a licensed and insured contractor.

Assignment of Lease-This provides for what conditions, if any, a Tenant can assign the lease to, say, a purchaser of the business. In most cases, but not all, once a lease is assigned, the original Tenant is no longer liable under the lease. A Landlord is not obligated to agree to an assignment clause, but when they do, there are usually significant conditions for the Landlord to agree. Some examples would be an increase in the Security Deposit and financial information from the assignee, to name two.

Sublet of Lease-This differs from an assignment as the original Tenant is still in "ownership" of the Lease and as such, is responsible in the event the Sub-Tenant does not perform. This will also usually require Landlord consent. The subtenant is basically "borrowing" all or part of the Demised Premises.

Defaults and Remedies-Every lease covers defaults and how to cure them. There are 2 basic types of defaults in a lease: monetary and non-monetary. Monetary is obvious. If you don't pay your rent or any other charges due under the lease, quite simply, you are in default. The lease will likely provide for a late fee in addition to the rent. If rent and all fees are not paid, the landlord will have the right to sue for the rent and possession of the space. Non-monetary defaults would be a default under any other provision of the lease. If the lease provides that you have to sign an estoppel certificate for a lender within 10 days and you don't, this would be an example of a non-monetary default. The lease will provide for cure periods so the tenant can get back in good graces with the landlord.

Insurance-In this litigious world, insurance is a major item in any lease. The landlord is going to insist that the tenant carry insurance, and most important, liability insurance, with the landlord being named additional insured.

There are literally dozens of other clauses in a commercial lease as well. They can easily run 30 pages or more. Items like Landlord access to space, indemnifications, rules of the property, default provisions and many more. You can Google commercial leases and find some examples online. Let's take a look at the commercial sub-types previously mentioned to give you a Back of the Napkin working knowledge.

Retail is probably the most complicated type of space

as there are many unique variables involved. Leasing the right space requires in-depth market knowledge, population and income demographics, traffic counts, and competition analysis. Sophisticated national retailers will create a pro-forma for every location they are considering. It will take into account sales projections, occupancy costs, labor costs and profit projections. Does the potential location have adequate road frontage for exposure? Does the property offer adequate signage? Is the property on the "going to work side of the street" or the "coming home side?" For example, if you are a Starbucks, you would be looking for that going to work side of the street.

There are numerous categories of retail tenants. It is important to understand the differences and the role each plays:

Anchor tenants-In a strip shopping center, supermarkets and DIY (do it yourself), i.e., Home Depot or Lowes, usually function as an anchor. The anchor tenant(s) serve as the main draw to the center as those types of tenants create significant foot traffic, which benefits the smaller tenants, also known as satellites. They typically lease large spaces, anywhere from 50,000-150,000 square feet. A local supermarket chain may lease smaller spaces depending on their model. Anchor tenants typically pay a lower rent per square foot than the smaller tenants for a number of reasons. Firstly, an anchor tenant is important for the success of the shopping center as it serves as a draw, and the landlord needs to incentivize the tenant to be part of the project. Further, as they are leasing a significant piece of space, they are entitled to a "volume" discount. Landlords may also do some tenant improvements for an anchor or provide a tenant improvement (TI) allowance of X dollars per square foot. The anchor typically signs a long-term lease, say 20-25 years in base term. In malls, the typical anchor has traditionally been department stores. The mall shopping experience is vastly different than of the strip center. The mall-shopper is a more casual, relaxed experience where time is not necessarily a factor. As there are usually multiple varieties of, say, fashion and shoes, for example, the shopper can browse and comparison shop. The strip center focuses more on the daily necessities, like a supermarket, dry cleaner, and a number of casual dining options like pizza and Chinese. When a shopper goes to a supermarket, they typically do not go to other stores in the center on the same trip, as the supermarket shop normally includes some perishables, like milk or ice cream. The customer gets used to seeing the other tenants in the center when they go to the supermarket, so the hope is they will return to use those shops or go to one, like the dry cleaner, before they do the supermarket shopping.

Satellite tenants-These are the smaller tenants in the shopping center that feed off of the foot traffic from the anchor tenant(s). They typically are approximately 1,000-5,000 square feet. They pay the highest rent per foot in order to be in a center with the anchor(s).

National vs. Local Tenants-National tenants are those that have multiple stores regionally or nationally, such as CVS Drugs, McDonald's, Dollar General, Starbucks, TJ Max and Auto Zone, to name a few. The appeal of these tenants to a landlord is great. Firstly, they are what are known as credit tenants as you can literally take their lease to the bank to help procure financing. Historically this type of tenant does well, and their brand names have mass appeal. The rents they will pay vary greatly by category. Local tenants are exactly as they are named. Local retailers may own one or several shops locally. They pay higher rents than the National tenants as the risk the landlord takes is higher, as the failure rate among local tenants is much greater than the National tenants. They are usually smaller tenants, such as a liquor store or dry cleaner. Most centers will have a blend of local and National tenants. Let's talk about franchises for a few minutes. As a franchisee, the owner basically owns one store in the beginning but gets the advantage of name recognition and years of know-how and expertise. Sources indicate that franchises have a lower failure rate than independently owned stores. This will naturally vary from franchise to franchise, but when was the last time you saw a closed McDonald's. In addition to brand recognition, franchises offer a high level of training and know-how. Store layouts, sources of inventory, power in numbers with advertising, prepackaged signs and promotional boards, to name a few. If considering a franchise, you will want to get a copy of the Franchise Disclosure Document or FDD. This contains an enormous amount of information, including how many stores were opened and very importantly, how many stores have closed. By law, you will get all financial data on the franchisor. It has copies of all documents that the franchisee will be required to sign and lays out all costs and fees, including potential costs of opening the store. This document typically is 100+ pages and is a must-read for any potential franchisee.

Unanchored centers, meaning no large tenant presence, flourish as well. This type of center normally serves as a specific area or neighborhood offering convenience with proximity to where people live. This type of center usually contains those tenants that service daily needs, like a dry cleaner, a delicatessen, and possibly a local drug store, although there are fewer these days, as the big drug store chains dominate the market. The ideal size of this type of center is approximately 10,000 to approximately 25,000 square feet. Anything over 25,000 square feet to, say, 60,000 square feet is a dangerous size in my experience. That size center is too large to fill with local tenants as they just don't exist and too small to house an anchor, which, as I pointed out, pays a lower per-square-foot rent and still leaves room for higher-paying satellite tenants. Occasionally, you may find a smaller local or ethnic supermarket that may take 25 to 30,000 square feet, but this is less common.

Factory Outlet centers are another type of shopping center. A true factory outlet center has stores that are run by the actual brand manufacturers such as Samsonite and London Fog for example. They sell directly to the public at discount prices, as they are eliminating the wholesaler and the retailer. Historically, the concept was to create factory outlet centers in rural areas a certain distance from malls and department stores so as to appear they are not competing with the stores they sell to. They are very popular across the country. To some degree, they have evolved into a hybrid as there is a mix of true manufacturers stores and some traditional retailers. You will see this in some of the Tanger Outlet Centers.

Many shopping centers also contain pad sites, also known as out parcels. These are pieces of land that house free-standing buildings that can be part of a shopping center. Pad site tenants typically have a drive-through, like fast food and drug stores. All the drug chains have been moving from in-line stores to pad sites, or free-stand stores, in order to have a drive-through. When drive-throughs first hit the scene, I found it very perplexing as to what the thinking was, as it basically kept the customer out of the store, thus eliminating any impulse purchases. I was told that once one of them did it, they all had to follow suit. It does offer convenience for the customer, which is a benefit. Virtually all of the fast-food chains are on pad sites for the same reason. Occasionally, a fast food or drug will be in line in a market where no free stands are available or in a unique market that they don't want to pass up.

Retail leases will contain numerous provisions generally unique to retail:

Signage Clause-This will specify where signs can go. At the least, one would want signage over their storefront. If there is a pylon sign, tenants always want to be on that as well. The larger, national tenants will get priority if space is limited, which it usually is. The clause will discuss sign size and, in some cases, even sign colors. Of course, signage will be subject to town approval, which it commonly is.

Use Clause-As previously mentioned, this clause is very important in retail. Most shopping centers, other than very large centers and malls, do not allow for duplication of uses in order to increase the odds of success for the tenants. If the tenant is a card store, the use clause will say something like "for use as a card store, carrying those items customarily sold in a card store in the N.Y. metropolitan area," and no other use. This is very specific and clear. A tenant can't wake up one morning and decide to become a clothing shop if their use clause is for a card store.

Exclusivity Clause-In many cases, the tenant will be granted exclusivity for their use. This stops other tenants in the same property from competing with them. The exclusivity clause will generally exempt a large tenant like a supermarket or department store. In many cases, you will see a greeting card section in a supermarket, even if the card store has exclusivity. Those larger tenants, also known as anchor tenants, don't want to be bound by the smaller tenant's exclusivity. Even with exclusivity, there will inevitably be some product overlaps between tenants. A hair salon, although primarily a hair cutter, will also typically sell some products like shampoo, which will also be sold in a health and beauty aid store. In those cases, the salon may be restricted to selling those products in X square feet or less.

CAM (or common area maintenance clause)-As you are aware, shopping centers have common areas that all the tenants share. Parking lots and sidewalks make up the bulk of common areas in a strip center. The cost of maintaining these areas is commonly borne by the tenants. This is usually done based on pro-rata share. This is calculated by dividing the tenant's demised premise square footage into the total shopping center size. If a tenant occupies 5,000 square feet in a 100,000-square-foot shopping center, then the tenant has a pro-rata share of 5%. In that case, the tenant would be responsible for 5% of the CAM expense. Typical CAM expenses would include parking lot maintenance, snow removal, parking lot lighting costs, landscaping and maintenance of any other features, such as water features for decorative purposes. There is no hard and fast rule on which expenses a landlord may attempt to include in CAM. In general, capital improvements, such as replacing a roof are not included in CAM. Some landlords will add an administrative fee to the CAM. Larger national tenants will usually push back on this as they see this as the landlord turning CAM into a profit center.

Percentage Rent-Occasionally, Landlords will agree to give a national credit-worthy tenant a lower base rent in exchange for Percentage Rent. In this scenario, a Tenant will pay an agreed % amount of sales volume when the sales volume exceeds a certain level. This can be either an arbitrary, negotiated sales volume or what is known as a natural break point. As this can be confusing, let me give you an example. Let's say the tenant agrees to pay a percentage rent of 3% over the natural break point. Let's also say the Tenant is paying $10.00 per square foot on 100,000 square feet. The sales volume would need to reach a level that the base rent would be 3% of that volume. The annual base rent in this example is $1,000,000. (100,000 square feet X $10.00 per square foot). The formula for the natural break point would be the annual base rent divided by the percentage of rent agreed. In this case, it would be $1,000,000 /.03. This would mean the Tenant needs to reach a sales volume of $33,333,333.3 before percentage rent kicks in. The Tenant would then be responsible for a 3% percentage rent over that volume. This may sound impossible, but it is not. A large anchor tenant is capable of producing volumes at and higher than this level.

Let's move on to office buildings:

Office buildings are generally ranked into 3 classes:

Class A office buildings are the cream of the crop. These are newer or newly renovated buildings in excellent locations. They offer amenities, such as a fitness center, on-site dining venue(s), have the latest in technology, possibly a media center, and have state of the art finishes. Needless to say, they come with a higher price tag per square foot. Tenants concerned with image and location gravitate to these properties.

Class B buildings are mid-range buildings, usually older, but offer some basic amenities, such as a coffee shop and possibly a fitness room if the building is large enough. Rents are reflective of this and are somewhat lower.

Class C buildings are usually significantly older, probably in need of some updating and upgrading, probably are in an inferior location, and usually offer the most competitive rents.

Keep in mind that rating these buildings is somewhat subjective and will vary by market. What may be a class b building in one market may be the best building offered in a different market. Suffice it to say tenants will look at buildings based on their requirements and budget.

Office leases will uniquely contain the following:

Loss Factor-This is important to understand and critical to know how to do the calculation. I will Back of the Napkin the calculation to the best of my ability. Just like the lower the CAP rate, the higher the value, this will seem confusing at first, but I will unpack it for you. Office buildings are comprised of, you guessed it, offices. They also contain common areas as shopping centers do. These common areas are hallways, elevators, bathrooms accessible in the hallways, and lobbies, which are sometimes very spacious. The common area would be defined as any space in the office building not rented by a specific tenant. In a shopping center, as we discussed, the common areas are reimbursed to the landlord via CAM charges. It is done differently in an office building. Office buildings have what is known as a loss factor. Technically, the landlord would calculate the amount of square footage dedicated to the common areas and come up with a percentage. If a 100,000-square-foot building has 20,000 square feet of common area, then the loss factor would be 20%. Assuming a 20% loss factor, this means the tenant will pay rent on 20% more space than he is renting. This is known as rentable footage vs. usable. You would pay for 20% more space than you are actually getting to reimburse the landlord for the cost of operating and maintaining the common area space. Here is where it can get tricky. If you are renting 800 square feet, how many feet will you pay rent on, assuming a 20% loss factor? Invariably, those inexperienced in this, myself included, back in the day, get it wrong. The incorrect logic would be:

"Well, I am getting 800 square feet, and the loss factor is 20%, therefore, my rentable square footage would be 960 square feet, which is 20% more than 800."

This sounds good, but it is incorrect. The problem is

you are starting with the net number to determine the gross number. It needs to happen the other way around to arrive at the correct number. You will see this by the time we are done.

The proper way to "gross up" the square footage is as follows. If the loss factor is 20%, you take the inverse of that or 80%, and you divide the usable footage into this:

800 usable feet/.80=1,000 rentable square feet. You can now clearly see that 200 feet is the correct amount of footage that the tenant should pay for based on a 20% loss factor. Again, in general terms, the formula is:

Usable square footage divided by the inverse of the loss factor=rentable square footage. Another example:

The tenant is getting 1,200 usable square feet. The loss factor for the building is 25%. What is the rentable footage the tenant will pay for? Incorrectly, the novice would take 1,200 and add 25% to that to get 1,500 square feet (1,200 X.25=300).1,200 + 300=1,500.

The correct way to gross this up is:

1,200 square feet/ .75=1,600 rentable square feet. For the sake of sounding repetitive, you calculate rentable (or gross) footage by taking the usable (or net) footage and divide by the INVERSE of the loss factor.

Previously, I mentioned that the landlord

(theoretically) calculates the common area footage to determine the loss factor. This is not always the case. Sometimes, the loss factor may be significantly higher than the "market" loss factor. In other words, if buildings in a particular market are running an 18-20% loss factor, and a particular building has a 30% loss factor, which is possible, the owner may be forced to arbitrarily reduce the loss factor he is using on leases to be more competitive in the market.

At the end of the day loss factor is quite simple as long as you know the formula, and now you do!

Parking can be an issue in office buildings. Unlike shopping centers, which of course, have certain peak traffic times and days, office buildings go to virtually full occupancy, basically 5 days a week from 9-5 (roughly). This can lead to parking issues, as in addition to employees, there are visitors coming to an office building to be serviced. In order to attract a desirable tenant, the landlord may have to set aside reserved parking for that tenant. This can be problematic as it can lead to resentment from other tenants, and policing who is actually using the reserved parking is a problem. That said, it does occur often that a landlord will agree to reserved parking. This becomes a clause in the lease outlining how many and where those spots will be. The landlord will usually make it clear that the landlord is not responsible for policing or enforcing this, as it is virtually impossible.

Tenant Improvements-Unlike retail, where space is typically delivered "as is" or with minimal work done by the landlord (other than national credit-rated tenants), office space is usually built out by the landlord. As always, this is a matter of negotiation between the parties, but typically, office space is delivered ready for furniture installation. Most landlords have what is known as a "standard work letter," which includes items like carpet, paint, distribution of electrical outlets, partitioning, and sometimes plumbing for a kitchen or a bathroom. The lease will detail exactly what work the landlord is obligated to complete prior to the delivery of space. A detailed space plan will also be attached to the lease, showing what the finished space will look like.

Utilities-Unlike retail or industrial, individual offices are rarely separately metered. This is because in the office building world, tenants will come and go, and the defined area of any particular office is subject to change depending on the requirements of new tenants occupying the space. Typically, there will be a per-square-foot charge for utilities. In the Long Island market, it is typically $3.50-$4.00 per square foot. This will vary regionally based on utility costs in a particular area.

Let's look at Industrial buildings:

Industrial buildings have unique characteristics as well. This type of property helps support all aspects of the creation and storage of, well, everything. Being this is "Back of the Napkin" style, we will look at this category without getting too in-depth. Industrial buildings have sub-categories such as warehousing and manufacturing. Actual zoning categories will vary in each town and municipality. Unlike retail, location is not particularly important as there are no "retail" customers coming to these facilities. Industrial buildings have a language of their own:

Ceiling Height-This is important, especially in warehousing, as storage is measured in cubic feet. "Clear" or "Under Steel" ceiling height is the ceiling height from the floor, to the steel beams or any other item below the actual ceiling.

Loading Docks-As the name implies, these are used to load and unload trucks and often have an elevated concrete "dock" to facilitate the fact that the opening of trucks is usually about 4 feet above the ground.

Roll-Up Doors-Again, as the name implies, these are steel doors that roll up into a storage housing. This facilitates the ability to drive trucks directly into the warehouse space.

Manufacturing, as opposed to warehousing, usually has a separate zoning in most municipalities. Although both are considered industrial, manufacturing is more labor-intensive than warehousing, and manufacturing poses potential environmental issues. In some areas, there is a distinction between light industrial and heavy industrial. Heavy industrial, which is big-time manufacturing, such as autos, also require enormous amounts of electrical power. Floor loads, meaning the weight the floors can tolerate, can be a factor depending on the weight of equipment and the like. You will need to have that conversation with the landlord in advance.

Typically, industrial buildings have 15-20% of space dedicated to offices. Another category called Flex can be adjusted to have more space dedicated to offices. As industrial is less parking intensive than office or retail, the amount of parking provided according to code is less than the other two. Although location for industrial real estate is not as critical as retail, it is still important to be in close proximity to major roadways as Industrial processes require frequent deliveries and pickups by truck. Historically, industrial space was in lower demand. With the advent of ecommerce, industrial space has become in high demand and as such, rental rates have escalated significantly.

In an industrial lease there will be heavy attention paid to toxic substances and environmental indemnities. All the other lease clauses that are standard to leases will be contained in an industrial lease as well.

Back of The Napkin Summary-Leases

Leases are contracts. Contracts that will bind the parties for an extended period of time. It is important to have a competent attorney review a lease document thoroughly. If you are leasing space or if you are a broker assisting a client, it is important to set proper parameters in advance. Where do I need to be geographically? How many square feet do I need? You may need the assistance of a space planner or architect to determine this. In the office space world, most large office building landlords will provide that service to you once they have your requirements. How many private offices? What size conference room(s)? Do you need a small kitchen? How many desks are in the bullpen area, if being utilized? Do you need a storage room for supplies or documents? If so, approximately how big?

Space planning is the most intricate in the office space world. In the retail and industrial world, the space will be determined by what type of use you are creating. If it is a franchise situation, the franchisor will provide all details regarding store size and prototypes. With industrial, if it is warehousing, you need to know the quantity and size of items you will be warehousing. If the items are stackable, you can take that into account, as you may need fewer square feet if you can store them vertically. In manufacturing, equipment size and quantity need to be known to estimate space requirements. What is my budget? What work, if any, do I need the landlord to perform? Keep in mind that any landlord work can and usually will affect the rent you pay. When do I need the space? These and many other considerations are important to identify upfront.

In office leases, it is important to remember that the amount of space you pay for is usually not the same amount of space you get. That pesky loss factor comes into play, so in general, you can expect to pay for 10-20% more space than you will get.

In retail, the name of the game is location, location, location. If you are opening a store or a broker assisting a client, this is probably the most critical decision that you will make. Keep in mind most retail leases, other than credit tenants will provide that the space will be turned over as is, with little or no work. This is certainly negotiable and should be probed.

In industrial, items like ceiling height and availability of loading docks and roll-up doors could be important factors.

No matter what type of property you intend to lease, it is critical to do your homework and research every aspect. I may sound like a broken record, but once a lease is signed, the parties are obligated for, likely, many years.

Back of The Napkin Checklist-Leases

__Identify geographical boundaries desired.

__If retail, order demographics-1-,3-, and 5-mile radius.

__If retail, Check traffic count (State DOT Website)

__If office or industrial, create a space plan to determine the square footage needed.

__Create a space occupancy budget.

__Create a construction budget for improvements.

__Retain competent counsel.

__Work with an experienced commercial agent.

(answers in the back of the book)

1. What does CAM stand for?

2. What is CAM?

3. What is the formula for grossing up a lease?

4. What are the classes of office buildings?

5. What are 2 features unique to industrial buildings?

6. What is the formula for calculating % rent with a natural breakpoint?

7. What does clear ceiling height mean?

8. How are utilities generally paid for by tenants in an office building?

Back of The Napkin-Lease Process

The "Holy Grail" in leasing is rent per square foot. This is the only way to compare apples to apples. Rent per year or month is meaningless as every space can be a different size. To derive the rent per square foot, you would multiply monthly rent x 12 to derive an annual rent, then divide the annual rent by the space size. For example, if a space is 1,500 square feet and the monthly rent is $4,000, the calculation would be $4,000 X 12 months/1500 square feet. This would be $32.00 per square foot. One would use this number to compare to other spaces in the market.

As I pointed out in the last section, a lease is a long-term contractual obligation. One should not enter into this lightly. The process will vary to some degree depending on the property type. Retail will generally involve the most research as the location of any particular store is potentially critical to survival. Analyze demographic data to make sure the population you are looking for is in the ring you are considering. Don't settle for "good enough". There will be too much riding on this decision. If you are going with a franchise, as discussed before, they will provide excellent support and guidance on store location.

In the office space world, things are not as critical. With office space, a law firm, for example, will likely not succeed or fail based upon which office building they choose. That decision can be driven by things like building amenities or proximity to the owner's home(s). The same would apply to industrial space as most industrial applications are not customer-dependent.

Start the process by surrounding yourself with top-notch professionals regardless of the property type. A commercial real estate broker, accountant, and attorney to begin with. You may need the services of an architect depending on the complexity of your buildout.

The broker will do the initial research to find and qualify potential locations. Today, due to the Internet, principals and brokers alike can research potential properties to lease or buy. Loopnet.com is an excellent tool to use. Searching for property on LoopNet is free. They make their money by charging to post listings. Many, but certainly not all, commercial properties for lease or sale are posted on LoopNet. Good old-fashioned pounding the pavement can help to locate additional properties, as most times there are "for rent" signs somewhere on or near a building with vacancies. It is also important to work with a broker that subscribes to Costar. This is the gold standard in commercial real estate research. Many commercial brokers subscribe to this platform. It contains virtually all properties in a given region, whether they are on the market or not. It will also provide valuable comparables for a market to determine where the market rents actually are. This can provide valuable ammunition when negotiating with a landlord.

I strongly recommend seeing multiple spaces, even if you love the first one you see. It will be educational, at the least, and many times, there are tradeoffs of features that you can only realize by comparing spaces,

Don't view spaces alone. Take a trusted employee or your partners if you have any. Seeing a space through multiple sets of eyes serves as a safety valve, as things can be missed, or certain issues may be overlooked. After seeing a few, you can short list down to one or two. Based on market research you can then start to craft an offer.

Here is what a basic letter of intent would look like:

OFFER TO LEASE

Date: January 23, 2024

Re: **Letter of Intent to lease retail space located at real property located at: 123 Main Street, Anywhere USA**

We are pleased to present this offer to lease space at the above referenced property on behalf of the proposed tenant. Please find proposed terms meant to outline the business arrangement that tenant would like to proceed forward with:

PREMISES: Space number 101, which the parties agree is 1,000 square feet.

LANDLORD: Good Properties, LLC

TENANT: Dave Smith

USE: A stationery store, and for no other use.

STARTING BASE RENT: $20.00 per square foot, which equals $20,000 per annum payable in equal monthly installments of $1,666.66.

TENANT POSSESSION: January 1, 2016

TERM: 5 years plus 2 5-year options

INCREASE: 4% per annum

PRO RATA SHARE: The demised premises represents 10% of the total Gross Leasable Area of the above referenced property.

RE TAXES: Pro-rata share equal to 10% of the total real estate tax for the above referenced property. Taxes shall be paid monthly in addition to Base Rent. Year 1 Real Estate Taxes equals $300 per month.

CAM: N/A

TI WORK: Tenant agrees to accept the premises AS IS.

ELECTRICITY: Separately metered

SECURITY DEPOSIT: $3,333.33, which equals 2 months base rent.

The above is not intended to be contractual in nature, or to set forth all of the relevant business terms and conditions that will be included in a lease but is intended to be an expression of the general business terms and conditions upon which landlord is willing to proceed with.

_____   _____

Landlord   Tenant

Keep in mind this is a basic letter of intent that would need to be tailored to each offer and will vary by property type. The word format of this document, which is customizable, is available for free at www.backofthenapkin.biz

This will begin the negotiation phase of the process. Depending on how aggressive your offer is and how motivated the landlord is, this could be a quick or drawn-out process. Patience is key as FOMO (fear of missing out) can set in. Your broker should be able to guide you through that process. I would not utilize an attorney for this negotiation. The most important business issues are base rent per square foot, as this is your comparison barometer, rent increases, keeping in mind nothing is carved in stone, tenant improvements that a landlord may pay for, use clause (especially retail) and exclusivity (mostly retail). A motivated landlord will do more than you think to procure a tenant. Keep in mind this is a non-binding letter of intent. This will be the basis for the lease, which will be a far more involved document that your attorney will review in detail. Be aware that some attorneys will try to show off their supposed prowess by trying to re-negotiate the business terms of the deal. Be careful with that, as they can renegotiate you right out of the deal. I have seen this happen.

The landlord's attorney typically provides the lease document and will review this with the tenant's attorney. Egos on both sides can get in the way. The client must keep control of this and speak up when they feel the attorney is overstepping or overreaching. There will likely be several redlined document drafts before reaching a signable lease.

Back of The Napkin Summary-The Lease Process

The "Holy Grail" in leases is the rent per square foot. It is the basis of comparison for other spaces in the market. Market research is key to exploring as many available space options as possible. The assistance of a good commercial real estate broker is key, especially one with access to Costar. Choose as many suitable locations as you like and go see them all. This will help you identify what is more important and what is less important. Short list down to 1 or 2 and submit letters of intent. Keep in mind, you can negotiate on more than one location before you decide. Don't be afraid to negotiate. My wife Linda always says, "If you ask for something and they say no, you won't grow a wart on your nose!" You may be able to extract a yes on something else for each no you get.

A good attorney on your team is critical. Make sure they have experience with commercial real estate leases. It is a complicated business.

Back of The Napkin Checklist-The Lease Process

__Leave adequate time to see spaces.

__Have a second or third pair of eyes to view spaces.

__Retain competent counsel.

__Draft complete letters of intent.

__Create a construction budget for improvements.

__Work with an experienced commercial agent.

(answers in the back of the book)

1. Who typically provides the lease document?

2. What is a critical member of your team in the lease process?

3. What is a typical security deposit?

4. does the landlord have to put security from a commercial lease in escrow?

5. When does a lease typically commence?

Back of The Napkin-Sales Technique

A Little Background

I feel a bit of my history is warranted here. I will do my best not to bore you! Hang in there; I promise it will be worth it. I owe my success in almost everything I did to the techniques I will share with you. I graduated college in 1976 with a degree in Secondary Education-Social Studies. It worked out well for me that it was the single worst year for graduating teachers in decades. I sent 200 requests for applications. Requests for applications, mind you, not applications. I got back one application to teach at a private school in Pennsylvania, paying $6,000 per year. I grant you 1976 is a while back, but still-$6,000 dollars!!! I hit the want ads, yes, the want ads! In those days, you looked for jobs in a newspaper. Indeed! Pun intended. My favorite radio station at the time was WBAB Radio in Babylon, N.Y. They had an ad for selling radio advertising, commission only. I was still living at home, with my folks, with all the comforts, so I figured, why not?

We all start somewhere. On the first day on the job, I showed up, and they gave me a folder of blank contracts and I was told to hit the road and sell. That was truly the extent of my training. They gave me a rate card and told me I must stick to those rates per minute. Granted, I was not lacking in self-confidence, as is still the case today, but where do I start? Most of the other salespeople were not about to help me as this was a competitive business. I went on my merry way going into small businesses, asking for the owner, and about half the time the owner was in. I proceeded to tell them what a great station WBAB is. I told them how our advertising worked. I told them about the demographics of our listeners. Yup, I was telling them everything and not making a single sale. After all, what did I know about sales? I just came from an environment as an aspiring teacher where you spent the entire day telling students what they needed to learn. My dad was in sales and was very good at it. He worked in the garment district and sold ladies' loungewear, which was also a very competitive business. I told him how discouraged I was and was considering quitting, which goes against my DNA. He asked me to describe my presentation, which I did. He said, "So you are telling them all this-correct?" "Yes, I said." He said, "Let me ask you a question. Did you ask them anything? Did you ask them to describe their clientele? Did you ask them what other promotions or advertising they do? It was like an epiphany. I said to myself, "SHUT UP, stupid. Stop telling and start asking." I spoke to my sales manager at the time, and he helped me revamp my presentation. Between him and my Dad, I was onto something. I started asking and engaging, and yes-listening. My success started to come, slowly at first, and then consistently. I did OK but did not love the business. For me to be truly successful, I must love what I am doing. I decided to look at other opportunities. Again, dear old Dad came through and introduced me to an acquaintance who was a pharmaceutical company's district manager. G.D. Searle was a pharmaceutical giant back in the day. They had numerous successful prescription drugs and some well-known over-the-counter products like Dramamine and Metamucil. I need to finish my career path, and we will come back to my experience at Searle, which basically changed my life. (for the better lol). Waiting 45 minutes in each doctor's office just to get five or ten minutes with the doctor was way more than my type-A personality could stand. After my time in pharmaceuticals, I decided I did not want to work for anyone. I wanted to be in business on my own. I started looking at small businesses with a business broker (I use that term loosely, as in N.Y., anyone can call themselves a business broker, no license required!) I saw card stores, laundromats, delis, liquor stores and the like. Nothing was appealing to me. What did appeal to me was what the business broker was doing. Meeting new people every day, out in the field and most importantly, because of my training in pharmaceuticals, I knew I could be the best business broker out there. Thus, Eastern Business Exchange was born in Riverhead, N.Y. I had a cousin who owned a 2-story building on Main Street. Downstairs was a clothing store that he owned, and upstairs were small offices. Much to my dad's chagrin, Carl offered me a small office for $75 per month. My Dad was a good salesman, but he was old school. He was very nervous that I was giving up a good salaried position with a company car and expense account. It was a risk, but I was ready. I had business cards printed up, created some forms with the obvious required information and literally went door to door on Main Street, Riverhead. I asked each business owner if they were interested in selling their business. I was clueless about the process, but I figured how hard it could be? A bar owner a few doors down from my office said yes, and I was ecstatic. He gave me a tour of the place and when we were in the kitchen, he was showing off his new Ansul system. I had no idea what he was talking about. All I could say was, yeah, it's a beauty, as I was looking around the kitchen having no idea where it was! Needless to say, the first thing I did after the appointment was to find out what an Ansul system was. Just to answer your now raging curiosity, it is a fire suppression system made for restaurant kitchens. I ran an ad in Newsday, and lo and behold, I found a buyer! I went to the contract signing expecting to get paid, and the attorney looked at me like I had two heads. He said, "You get paid at the closing!" I asked, "When will that be?" he said once the buyer gets his liquor license. I said oh, how long will that take? He said about 6-9 months; at that point, I realized I couldn't list any more businesses requiring liquor licenses, or I would be out of business. As I was clueless on all of this, it was truly a trial by fire and a very good argument as to why business brokers should have to be licensed! I grew Eastern Business Exchange and had two offices, one in Riverhead and one in Hauppauge, about 35 minutes west. Occasionally, I sold a business with the building, and I found that very appealing. Business brokerage was an easy transition into real estate. By pure coincidence, I attended a Yellow Pages seminar. Most of you probably have no clue what Yellow Pages is (or was). This was a business directory actually printed on yellow paper. There, I met Bill Bendernagel, who ran commercial brokerage for Merrill Lynch Realty. The name recognition of Merrill Lynch was very appealing to me as it sounded a lot better than Eastern Business Exchange. Plus, I would be handling real estate, which was my goal at that point. He convinced me to join him in running the division. He was a true mentor when it came to commercial real estate, and together, we grew the division on Long Island to 4 offices with over 100 agents handling commercial real estate and business brokerage. I trained them all with the techniques I learned at Searle. He truly helped me bring my career to the next level, and he was a great person. I was then recruited to be a partner in a startup business brokerage and commercial real estate company, Manheim Realty, where I was made a partner. I trained and nurtured scores of real estate agents. I was then recruited by a major Long Island developer, Vincent Polimeni, where I became a partner as well. I trained hundreds of agents and eventually became president of Polimeni International, where I was responsible for a portfolio of 3 million square feet of commercial property. We had office buildings and shopping centers on the East Coast. I was responsible for property management, leasing, training, procuring financing and development work. As I mentioned earlier, through my brother, we met an individual who owned land in Poland. We went over to see it. The site was not appropriate for a retail center (maybe a Factory outlet center someday), but we were amazed at the open-arms attitude we received regarding development. My observation after our first visit was that Poland needed a good public relations firm. The image most people have is so far from reality. Vibrant cities, beautiful countryside, historic towns with magnificent architecture and a population that is motivated to get things done. We went on to develop six enclosed malls over the next ten years. This was the most exciting period of my career. Overall, I have been truly blessed in my career and was fortunate enough to meet some really great people along the way. Since 2008, I have been on the Board of Directors for Hanover Bank in Mineola, N.Y. I serve as chairman of the credit committee, which reviews loans on a weekly basis. I am also a partner in Realty Connect, USA. My role in the company is to train and assist agents with their commercial transactions.

Now that you have a snapshot of my career, let's get back to Searle and my training.

I was hired, and completely contrary to my 0 training in radio advertising, I began a month-long training program that involved two weeks at the labs in Skokie, Ill, two weeks back in N.Y. in the field with a very experienced "detail man". The first two weeks in Illinois we spent 0 time on product knowledge, which was surprising. We spent the entire two weeks on, you guessed it, sales technique. I am not overstating the case when I say this experience was transformative. This set me up for the rest of my career, which is now about 45 years. Oy, I am getting old!! We role-played day after day. We were taught by some of the industry's best trainers.

Sell Me the Pen

Based on that training, one of the exercises I have used countless times is "sell me the pen". We would role-play and videotape each role-play so we could review and critique. With no warning or preparation, I would pick one of the students and hand him a pen as I proclaimed: sell me the pen. In all the years and countless times I did this, no one truly got it right. It usually started with that "deer in the headlights" face. The student would introduce himself as so and so from the Acme Pen Company, and I had the role of the buyer of supplies for Jones and Company. The salesperson would then invariably launch into a dialogue of all the reasons I should buy the pen.

"This is a great pen that will last a long time," "This pen is comfortable in your hand., "This pen is very stylish", and so on. The whole time, I would sit there with my hand on my chin, saying, "Uh-huh". I would let this go on for a few minutes, intentionally wanting the presenter to be as uncomfortable as possible, as this was part of the learning experience. Nothing they did invoked a response from me, so they had nowhere to go. I would then trade places. I became the salesperson for Acme Pens, and they became the representative of Jones and Company:

I started:

Good day, I am Philip Okun from Acme Pen Company. I am here today to show you our new line of quality pens with the intention of having your company purchase them. Let me ask you a question, "what is it you look for when you are purchasing pens for your company?" As the buyer would answer I am writing down the responses. I then repeated back his responses. "So, you need a pen that is reliable and cost-effective, as you use many of them." I then ask, "What else do you look for when purchasing pens?" The response is, "Those are the two most important things to me." I proceeded to make a presentation based on those two responses I received. "Based on the studies we did, we found Acme Pens to be virtually one hundred percent reliable. Based on that, we offer a 6-month guarantee on every pen. Further, since you will be purchasing large quantities, you will receive our biggest discount". How does that sound? The response is, "Sounds good." "Based on that, shall I start to process your order?" Sure, let's do it!

Can you see the difference between what the salesperson did initially versus this presentation? The salesperson who went first was out in the dark. He tried to use any features he could think of to sell the pen. What is the most important thing I did in my presentation? I started by asking questions. More importantly, I only used what are known as open-ended probes. Open-ended probes require an answer other than yes or no. Yes or no questions don't yield information. This one paragraph can help make you as successful as you want to be. We are going to dissect it in detail:

The process is based on a 5-step model:

1. State the Goal

2. Probe

3. Present

4. Trial Close

5. Close

We will now dissect the above presentation step by step:

State the Goal

"Good day, I am Philip Okun from Acme Pen Company. I am here today to show you our new line of quality pens with the intention of having your company purchase them."

I introduced myself, and I stated my goal. This is a crucial first step, so the path is clear. It is also very simple. As Yogi supposedly said, "If you don't know where you are going, you won't know when you get there." It reached a point where before any meeting, any phone call, business or personal, I would stop for 30 seconds and ask myself. What is the goal of this interaction? It eventually became automatic, and to this day, I ALWAYS consider what the goal is before I dive in. By stating the goal, you set the table, and you set expectations. It does not matter whether you sell real estate, widgets, or cars. Unfortunately, most (not all) car salesmen just want you to hear what they have to say. Some other examples of stating goals:

"It is my intent to find out what is important to you regarding your new home and show you at least 3 listings."

"My goal is to help you quantify the amount of space you will need for your new offices and show you at least two buildings."

"I am here today to show you our line of inkjet printers so I can fill your needs."

As long as you think about what your goal is, you can craft a sentence or two to express it.

Probe

"Let me ask you a question: what is it you look for when you are purchasing pens for your company?" As the buyer would answer I am writing down the responses. I then repeated back his responses. "So, you need a pen that is reliable and cost-effective, as you use many of them." I then ask, "What else do you look for when purchasing pens?"

If you were allowed only to have one take away from this section; this is it. Open-ended probing. This type of probing takes all the guesswork out of sales. Your customer is doing the work for you. By getting the information on what is important to them, you know exactly where to go in your presentation. You NEVER want to use a closed-end probe until you reach the close or if you are qualifying objections, which we will cover in a bit. Until then, you are engaging, writing down responses and re-engaging based on the answers you get. I am a firm believer in writing responses for two reasons. Firstly, it shows the client that you value their responses. Secondly, we are all human, and as such, we sometimes forget. If you have a written list of 3 things your client told you were important, you can't forget any of them.

Any question that gets a yes or no answer can be transformed into an open-ended probe.

"Did you like the property I just showed you?" **Closed end.**

"What did you like about the property I just showed you?" **Open ended.**

"Do you like blue cars?" **Closed end.**

"What color cars do you like?" **Open ended.**

"Would you like an office with a kitchen in it?" **Closed end.**

"What features would you like your new office to have?" **Open ended.**

It is not rocket science. The art of selling is getting as much <u>information</u> as possible. You never have to guess if you know.

Present

"I proceeded to make a presentation based on those 2 responses I received. "Based on the studies we did, we found Acme Pens to be virtually one hundred percent reliable for that reason. We offer a 6-month guarantee on every pen. Further, since you will be purchasing large quantities, you will receive our biggest discount".

If you probe properly and you know your product well, your presentation becomes easy whether you are selling property, widgets, cars, or anything else. If you probed properly, you know exactly what features and benefits to highlight. You have written down what is important to the client, and you should address them one by one.

Along the way, in your presentation, something new may come up. It could be a legitimate concern, or it could be a smoke screen. I refer to legitimate concerns as alligators or objections, and as such, we have Okun's Dictum I. "You can't drain the swamp once you are up to your butt in alligators". In other words, don't ignore or skip over an objection. You need to qualify it and then resolve it, and move on.

"I also need my pens to be stylish". My response would be: "You expressed that you need pens that are reliable and cost-effective. If I show you a pen that is also stylish but more expensive, would you be interested?" This is intentionally a closed-end probe to help the customer prioritize their needs. "No…..I guess stylish is not that important", the customer says. You have helped the customer with priorities, and you eliminated the issue.

Trial Close

"How does that sound? "

Very simple open-ended probe. Another trial close would be something like: "What else can I answer for you in order to make a decision?" Again, open-ended and looking for any additional input. The trial close is intended to help tidy things up prior to asking for the business. It helps the client get comfortable with the decision he is about to make. If the client is not comfortable for any reason, you will find out why.

Close

"Based on that, shall I start to process your order?"

This is the final step in the process. The customer had responded to the trial close with "sounds good" so now is the proverbial moment of truth. This is when you want to use closed-end probes. No beating around the bush with this.

At the risk of sounding redundant, the whole key to this model is open-ended probing. You don't offer anything about your product or services until you know what is important to the client. It makes your life so much easier as there is no guesswork. It is critical not to lose sight of the fact that the close has to be aligned with the goal, especially in real estate, which is a multi-stage process. You don't go from a phone call to the closing table in one shot. If you are canvassing for listings on the phone, what is the goal? Ideally, to get an appointment. Your probing and presentation are designed to get you the appointment, nothing more. Make sure you internalize that before you begin. In a typical real estate transaction, there will be multiple interactions all with different closes. Combine them all, and you end up at the closing table. I strongly suggest practicing with the model. It will be awkward at first, but once you get used to it, it becomes second nature. You can role-play with a colleague and videotape it so you can critique it. Use any product you want. Pens, milk, cell phones. The product does not matter, but the process does. I sat at the breakfast table and role-played with myself using milk.

1. State the Goal

2. Probe (open-ended probes)

3. Present

4. Trial Close (open-ended probe)

5. Close (closed-end probe)

Memorize and, more importantly, use it. I can tell you from 45 years of experience it truly works.

Let's go back to probing for a minute. (You think it's my favorite part of this?) If you start your questions with what, where, when, who, how, and why, you can't go wrong. If your question starts with is, do or did, you are heading toward closed-end land.

Open

When you are looking for a new car, what is important to you?

What are you looking for in your new office space?

What is your timing to take occupancy?

How do you plan to finance this purchase?

Who would you like to bring with you on the second showing?

What is a good time to meet?

Closed

Did you like the property we just saw?

Is this a good time to talk?

Do you want to be in Suffolk County?

Hopefully, it is clear that closed-end probes will lead to a dead end and yield no usable information. I have always said that just about every situation in life is a selling situation. Take the example of the husband fighting with the wife:

"John, I want you to put your clothes in the hamper," says Mary. (state the goal)

"Why don't you put your clothes in the hamper? "(open-end probe)

John responds, "It is too dark on the left side of the closet, so I can't see." Mary says she will move the hamper and does. (presentation, in this case, is an action-moving the hamper).

Mary asks, "What else do I need to do to get you to use the hamper?" (trial close)

John says, "Nothing."

Mary says, "OK, John, will you please use the hamper?" (close)

As silly as that may sound, that interaction and most interactions in life require a give and take. Using the model increases the likelihood of a positive outcome immeasurably.

Now, who would think a simple argument between a husband and a wife could be resolved with the sales model I shared with you? The proof is right here. Practice the model and memorize it. Consciously go through the steps the next time you are with a client. Your success in sales is right in this chapter!

One more point I would like to make. I just finished reading the book written by Jeopardy mega-champion Amy Schneider, titled "In the Form of a Question." Excellent book. The book has 22 chapters, all chapter titles being, of course, in the form of a question. Guess what---21 of the 22 chapter titles are open-ended probes. Hmmmm…think about that when you are trying to build success in anything!

Back of The Napkin-Sales Technique-Review

(answers in the back of the book)

1. What is an open-ended probe?

2. When do you use a close-ended probe?

3. During probing, what action should you take when the customer is responding to his needs?

4. Why is it important to state the goal?

5. What are alligators? (no, not the animal!!)

6. What is Okun's dictum 1?

7. What is the art of selling?

Epilogue

We covered a ton of ground on our **Back of the Napkin** journey. I hope you enjoyed reading it as much as I enjoyed writing it. I simplified all of this as best I could, and I believe accomplishing this in a book this size proves that. This business can be as simple or as complicated as one chooses. My career led to a level of success I had not imagined. Financially, I have no complaints. More than that, I had the privilege to train so many hundreds of agents and employees, always trying to help everyone find their best self. I have to say that I take great satisfaction in the success stories of those I have trained, and fortunately, there are many. In finishing this book, I want to quote my wife Linda, who tells me every time I go to tennis: Just do your best. That's all I ask. I leave the house inspired not just to win, but as she said: I strive to do my best, no matter what I am doing! Now go out and do your best!!

Feel free to email me anytime with any questions: philip@philipokun.com and visit our new website www.backofthenapkin.biz and join our community. Thank you!!

Back of The Napkin-Glossary

Acre- Contains 43,560 square feet.

Anchor Tenant- Large tenant in a shopping center. Usually, a supermarket or home improvement store in a strip shopping center. Mall anchors are typically department stores.

Annual Increases- The amount that base rent increases, usually on an annual basis, but this is subject to negotiation.

As of Right Use- This usually refers to land use. This is the type of use that the property is zoned for. This does not mean you can just pick up a shovel and start building. All permits and approvals are still required.

Assignment of Lease Clause- This clause defines the rights, if any, of the tenant to assign the lease to a third party. If a lease is assignable, it will usually be subject to landlord approval.

Base Rent-(Annual)- This is the amount of rent payable on an annual basis. It is calculated by multiplying the square footage of the demised premises by the base rent per square foot. Other charges such as real estate taxes or CAM may apply in addition to the base rent.

Base Rent/square foot- This is the amount of rent being charged per square foot of space in the demised premises.

CAM- (Common Area Maintenance)- Most common in retail and sometimes industrial this is the cost to maintain the common areas, such as parking lots, the roof, landscaping and snow removal to name a few. This cost is usually shared by the tenants of the property on a pro-rata basis.

Capitalization (CAP) Rate- This is a rate of return acceptable to an investor. Commonly applied when purchasing investment property.

Clear Ceiling Height- This is the ceiling height from the floor to the lowest impediments such as beams or the ceiling.

Commitment-(Mortgage)- This is a document specifying the terms and conditions upon which a lender will make a loan to a purchaser (borrower),

Competition Survey-Used in retail, this plots, on a map, all potential competition for a particular use. Informationally, the survey may show other significant retail in the area, even of different uses.

Contract of Sale- Document specifying the terms and

conditions upon which a buyer and seller will transact a piece of real estate.

Debt Service Coverage Ratio-(DSCR)- The ratio of debt to income that a lender will require. Typically, this will be 120%.

Demographics- Breakdown of characteristics of a population in a specific geographic ring. It can be by zip code or, more commonly, rings of 1 mile and up from the subject property. Typically, 1,3-,5- and 10-mile rings.

Demised Premises- Specific description of the premises being leased by a tenant. It will usually specify, by address, unit number and the square footage being leased.

Due Diligence- This is a process whereby a purchaser verifies information provided by a seller. Typically, leases and financial information provided are reviewed. A physical inspection and environmental review are also typically conducted.

Environmental Review- This is a process where a property is assessed for any environmental issues, such as toxic waste contamination (fuel leakage) or the possible presence of asbestos. A phase 1 environmental is a review of the history and records of the property, along with a visual inspection of the property by a company that specifically performs these reviews. Should there be anything suspicious, a phase 2 review, where ground samples are taken, may be ordered.

Exclusivity Clause- Gives a tenant exclusivity in a particular category. This may apply in retail centers and sometimes in office buildings where a doctor may get exclusivity for a particular type of medicine, i.e., Neurology.

Financing- Procurement of a loan, typically from a bank, but other sources are available as well.

Highest and Best Use- A term typically used by appraisers when valuing land, they will look at the highest and best use to calculate the potential value.

Goals- Levels of achievement. For goals to be valid, they must pass 3 tests. They must be realistic, challenging and measurable. Goal planning is critical to success on all levels.

Income/Expense Statement- Details the income and expenses of a commercial property. This will detail all income broken down by type, such as base rents, tax reimbursements, and any other additional rents. It will also detail all of the operating expenses of the property.

Lease Contract- A contractual document specifying the terms and conditions between a tenant and a landlord.

Lease Commencement- The date on which the lease

commences, and the 'clock' begins ticking on many terms of the lease. Commencement is usually upon occupancy by the tenant of the demised premises.

Lease Options- Periods of time in addition to the base term that may be part of a lease. Options can be for any specified period of time that the parties agree to.

Letter of Intent-Lease- A non-binding document specifying the major business terms of a lease. It is used by the attorneys as the basis for a lease, which is a binding contract.

Letter of Intent-Purchase- A non-binding document specifying the major business for the sale of a property. It is used by the attorneys as the basis for a sale contract, which is a binding contract.

Like Kind Exchange-(1031)- Upon the sale of a commercial property the seller commits to purchase another commercial property within 180 days. More detail can be found in the section Back of the Napkin-Tax Ramifications.

Loading Dock- A raised concrete platform in an industrial building utilized for the loading and unloading of trucks.

Loan to Value Ratio-(LTV)- The ratio of the mortgage to the value of the property established by appraisal.

Loss Factor- Office building term used to describe the difference between rentable footage and usable footage. The loss factor is intended to reimburse the landlord for the cost of maintaining the building's common areas.

Management Fees- The fee charged by a property management company for managing day to day operations of a property. In commercial real estate, it is typically a percentage of the gross building income.

Mortgage Contingency- A clause in a contract of sale making the closing contingent on the purchaser obtaining a mortgage to purchase the property. This clause will outline parameters such as the time frame to obtain a mortgage and the potential amount of the mortgage.

Multi-Family Property- A property comprised of apartments. If there are 4 or less apartments, it is considered residential property and as such, can be financed with residential mortgage financing. Any property with 5 or more apartments is considered commercial real estate.

National/Credit Tenant- This is a somewhat loose term to describe a retail tenant that has multiple locations, usually in a 'wide' geographic territory. Most importantly, their financial condition is such that banks will provide financing based on their lease.

Net Operating Income-(NOI)- This represents the gross income minus all operating expenses, such as real estate taxes, insurance, maintenance, etc. Debt service is NOT subtracted at this level. Net income before debt is the NOI.

Net Profit- This represents the NOI minus the debt service. Net Profit or Net Cash Flow is the money left after all expenses other than income taxes.

Operating Expenses- All expenses needed to operate the property other than debt service.

Pad Site- This is a piece of real estate in a shopping center that is not attached to the main building(s). A free-standing store such as drugs, fast food, or banks, for example. Typically, these pad site tenants require a drive-through window to service their customers.

Percentage Rent- Rent paid in addition to base rent. This percentage rent, as it denotes, is additional rent that is a percentage of sales above a certain breakpoint. The breakpoint can be arbitrary, as agreed, or it can be what is known as a Natural breakpoint. The formula to determine a Natural breakpoint is the percentage agreed upon divided by the annual base rent.

Prepayment Penalty- Typically found in commercial mortgages, this is a penalty for paying off the mortgage before its maturity. It can be a percentage agreed of the outstanding balance or, in some cases, what is known as yield maintenance. This can be very costly, as the lender is recovering all of the interest that would have been earned through maturity. This is common in CMBS mortgages, as those mortgages are pooled, tranched, and sold off as bonds.

Pro-Forma- Usually a spreadsheet showing projected rents and expenses over a period of time, usually years.

Purchase Money Mortgage- This is a mortgage held by the seller of the property. Keep in mind that on commercial properties, the buyer and seller can agree on negotiated terms. The laws for holding a mortgage on residential property vary, so check with a competent attorney.

Rent Commencement- In a lease agreement, there is what is known as Lease Commencement and Rent Commencement. They may or may not be the same. Typically, Rent Commencement is usually the later of occupancy or the completion of any rent concessions negotiated in the lease.

Roll up Door- Industrial buildings typically have this feature to allow trucks to be able to enter the building for loading and unloading.

Satellite Tenant- These are the "smaller" tenants in a shopping center. Unlike the anchor tenants, they pay higher rents per square foot. They rely on foot traffic generated by the anchor tenants.

Security Deposit- A sum of money deposited with the landlord to be used in the event a tenant does not pay rent or for use to repair any damages to the demised premises,

Sewage Treatment Plant (STP)- An on-site plant that treats the wastewater from the shopping center.

Small Business Administration-(SBA)- A government agency that provides various services to small businesses, including loans, disaster assistance and business counseling and training.

Square Foot- An area 12"x12". Real estate in the U.S. is measured by square footage. Rents are based on per square foot of space.

Sublet of Lease- An arrangement where a tenant sub-leases part or all of its space to a sub-tenant. The tenant on the lease is still responsible and liable for all payments and needs to ensure that the subtenant follows all rules and regulations of the building.

Survey- A drawing showing all boundaries and dimensions of a piece of real estate. All improvements on the property are also shown with dimension lines as well.

A licensed surveyor performs this service.

Tenant Improvements-(TI)- Modifications made to the Demised Premises. They can be done by either the landlord, the tenant, or a combination of both. This work and who is responsible for performing the work is clearly spelled out in the lease document. Plans and specifications are usually attached as well.

Term Sheet- Issued by a lender, the term sheet, as the name implies, spells out all terms and conditions of a proposed loan. A term sheet is NOT a commitment to make a loan, only an expression of interest subject to conditions spelled out.

Topographical Survey- This is a drawing showing all of the grade changes on a property. It is used to consider what grading needs to be done in order to construct improvements on the property.

Traffic Count- Measured in cars per day, and this is used particularly in retail to determine the level of traffic passing a particular site.

Upside Potential- Any number of factors can contribute to being able to enhance the value of a property. They include a building that is undersized based on the size of the land, leases with below market rents and tenants who may be month to month.

Use Clause- This denotes what a tenant can do in the demised premises. Particularly important in retail, in most cases, the tenant is restricted from doing anything other than their permitted use.

Vacancy Factor- A percentage of income determined by a bank that is deducted from the gross income, even if the property is fully rented.

Value Formula- Determining the value of a commercial property is accomplished by dividing a capitalization rate (CAP Rate) into the net operating income (NOI). This is somewhat arbitrary and is only a snapshot in time. If a property is vacant, pro-forma of potential value is utilized.

Zoning- All properties have a particular zoning denoting what the property can be used for. Changes in zone can be accomplished. This can be a time-consuming and expensive process, with no guarantee of a positive outcome.

The Holy Grails

I wanted to summarize for you my "Holy Grails" in commercial real estate:

Investment Properties: Net Operating Income, or NOI. It is the cornerstone of determining value. Apply a CAP rate or CAP rates for a range of values.

Land-Highest and Best Use-Regardless of zoning, what is the best use of this piece of land? This will be based on market conditions and research.

Leasing-Rent per square foot. This is the only way to compare apples to apples when looking at leasing space. Take the monthly rent, multiply it by twelve to determine annual rent, then divide by the number of square feet in the space to determine rent per square foot.

Back of The Napkin-Review Answers

Investment Properties

1. NOI

2. Under market leases and excess land

3. No

4. $4,457,142

5. No

6. Rent Roll, Income/Expense

7. Dance Wonder

8. In the event they take the property back, they will hire a management company

9. $5,000

10. The value increases

Vacant/Partially Vacant Properties

1. As an investor or a user

2. Assumptions and a pro-forma

3. No

4. LoopNet

Owner/User Properties

1. No

2. 1,3,5 and 10

3. SBA

4. yes

5. 51%

6. Higher cost

7. Yes

Land

1. Market research

2. A map showing the grade of the property

3. For visibility

4. The income produced

5. Architect, engineer, banker, attorney, broker

Purchase Process

1. Attorney & Broker

2. Never

3. A clause giving the borrower to procure a mortgage in order to close the transaction.

4. No

5. Review leases, review financial records, perform inspection, phase 1 environmental

6. Time is of the essence is risky for both parties

Financing

1. DSCR

2. Acquisition of real estate and equipment

3. Commitment

4. A penalty for prepaying a mortgage prior to the due date

5. The advantage of multiple sources of financing

6. Core samples to look for contaminants

7. More

8. Commercial Mortgage-Backed Securities

9. Higher LTV

10. Pre-leasing

Tax Ramifications

1. 39

2. Loss of Value

3. No

4. Deferral of capital gains tax

5. You have depreciation recapture

6. 45 days

7. You can depreciate 100% of the purchase price of the property.

8. 8-Qualified Intermediary.

Leases

1. Common Area Maintenance

2. The costs of maintaining common areas, including parking lot, roof, landscaping, snow removal

3. Usable footage divided by the inverse of the loss factor

4. A,B,C

5. Roll up doors, loading docks, high ceilings

6. Divide annual rent by the agreed percentage of rent

7. The height from floor to the lowest steel or roof

8. On a per square foot basis

Lease Process

1. Landlord

2. Attorney

3. 2 months' rent

4. No

5. Upon occupancy

Sales Technique

1. A question that does not evoke a yes or no answer

2. Close or qualifying an objection

3. Write them down

4. To establish a road map of where you are going

5. An objection

6. You can't drain the swamp when you are up to your butt in alligators!

7. Listening and using open end probes

About the Author

Philip A. Okun has been in the commercial real estate industry since 1981. He has expertise in leasing, sales, development, financing, and property management. He was president of Polimeni International, which owned and developed commercial properties in the U.S. and Poland. He oversaw a portfolio of office buildings and shopping centers in excess of 3,000,000 square feet. Additionally, he is a partner in Realty Connect USA Long Island. In that capacity, he trains agents that want to learn commercial real estate. Further, he is a founding director of Hanover Bank in Mineola, N.Y., which was created in 2008. He serves as chair of the loan committee and is a member of the audit, litigation, compensation, and fair housing committees. He is a licensed real estate broker in New York and Florida and was also a licensed Coast Guard commercial captain. He resides in West Palm Beach, Florida with his wife Linda.